GREAT BATTLES OF THE
CIVIL WAR

GREAT BATTLES OF THE
CIVIL WAR

SWAFFORD JOHNSON

Exeter Books

NEW YORK

A BISON BOOK

First published in U.S.A. in
by Exeter Books
Distributed by Bookthrift
Exeter is a trademark of Bookthrift Marketing, Inc.
Bookthrift is a registered trademark of Bookthrift
Marketing, Inc.
New York, New York

ISBN 0-671-06987-X

Printed in Hong Kong

Reprinted 1987

Page 1: Sherman's
March to the Sea, 1864,
from a contemporary
engraving.
Page 2-3: *Assault on Fort
Sanders*, a lithograph of
1891.
This page: The Union
Line at Nashville,
Tennessee, December
1864.

CONTENTS

The Battle of Fort Donelson, Tennessee (16 February 1862), a Union victory that led to Ulysses S Grant's promotion to major general and his nickname of 'Unconditional Surrender' Grant.

CHAPTER ONE
SUMTER FALLS
THE OPENING ACT

IF WAR IS 'A CONTINUATION of political relations by other means,' then it may also be said that once the first battle is fought, political relations have failed. Never was this maxim truer than with the opening shots of America's Civil War: decades, even centuries, of political relations had preceded the events that led to Fort Sumter, thus giving the battle a significance far beyond its brief duration, modest firepower and almost nonexistent casualty list.

The Civil War arose from a complex of problems – political, philosophical, economic and moral – that had haunted the United States from the beginning, implicitly from their first days as colonies and explicitly from their inception as a nation. These problems rolled through the years of the nineteenth century, gaining momentum, swelling until they had grown beyond the control of even the wisest of people.

Chief among these problems – or at least the one that proved to be the breaking point – was the institution of human slavery imposed upon black people (which endured in America longer than in any other Western nation). By the mid-19th century, slavery had been eliminated throughout the North, but was maintained in the South with a tenacity that was only partially explainable by slavery's support of the cotton economy. The other major problem festering over the years was that of federalism versus states' rights: federalism, strongest in the North, proclaimed the primacy of the Federal Government; states' rights doctrine, dominant in the South, upheld the primacy of each state's government.

These and related problems had tended increasingly to split the country along sectional lines. So it was that in the early spring of 1861 the volatile spirit of sectionalism came to its long-feared explosion point: when the wisest of people cannot solve a nation's problems, they must often be solved by the strongest, and great suffering results.

In the midst of this crisis, the most serious in the nation's history, the man whose election helped to precipitate it was inaugurated President. Elected by less than 50 percent of the voters, Abraham Lincoln came to the White House largely untried in national politics – an unknown quantity. Even before he arrived in Washington in February 1861, Lincoln faced the prospect of dealing with a rival government that was already claiming all Federal property within the boundaries of seven Southern states – South Carolina, Mississippi, Florida, Alabama, Georgia, Louisiana and Texas. After the November 1860 election these states had seceded from the Union and now called themselves the Confederate States of America. They had assembled their own representatives, who drew up a Constitution and selected a President – Jefferson Davis, a former Secretary of War in Washington. In his first inaugural address Lincoln repudiated the Confederate claim, vowing to 'hold, occupy, and possess' all Federal property. He made it clear that secession would not be tolerated.

Most significant among the Federal properties claimed by the Confederates were symbols of Federal power: four garrisons – three in Florida, far from the centers of government, and one in South Carolina. By the end of 1860, the attention of the entire country was riveted on the latter garrison – Fort Sumter, in Charleston Harbor. As early as 26 December 1860, the Federal commander there,

Below: The capture of insurrectionist Nat Turner, a radical slave preacher who led a pre-Civil War uprising of Virginia slaves and was executed with 12 of his followers.
Right: Fort Sumter, Charleston Harbor, the Federal garrison seized by Confederate soldiers in the first action of the war.

Major Robert Anderson, had withdrawn troops from the even more vulnerable Fort Moultrie, also in the harbor, and moved them to Sumter. At the beginning of 1861 this garrison, a pentagonal fort occupying an artificial island just off-shore, was unfinished, poorly armed, understaffed and running low on food. In January a provision boat sent by then President Buchanan had been fired on and turned back. Since then the Confederates had erected a semicircle of batteries on the mainland and islands around the fort. The Federals inside had done what they could to prepare for battle.

Both Secretary of State Seward and aging general-

in-chief Winfield Scott pressed Lincoln to evacuate Sumter. The President decided on 29 March 1861 neither to evacuate nor to reinforce the garrison, but to send a ship with provisions for the soldiers. On April 6 Lincoln advised South Carolina's governor of this order; he was making sure that the next critical step, an act of aggression, would have to be taken by the South.

Next day the Confederate commander in Charleston, General P G T Beauregard, cut off communications between Charleston and Sumter. Events accelerated, pulled on by the seemingly irresistible magnet of war. On 8 April the Confederacy organized its forces in the harbor. Two days later Beauregard was instructed by the Confederate Government to demand the fort's surrender and evacuation; the demand was presented to Major Anderson on 11 April. Anderson replied that he would evacuate on 15 April unless he were attacked or received further orders from Washington. This last stipulation did not satisfy the Confederates.

At 3:20 in the morning on 12 April, Anderson received a note from Beauregard's messengers: 'We

Above: Major Robert A Anderson, commander of Federal troops at Fort Sumter.
Left: General P T Beauregard, who designed the battle flag of the Confederate Army.
Below: The first inauguration of Abraham Lincoln, 4 March 1861. In remarks directed at those states voting for secession, Lincoln stated that 'The Union of these States is perpetual.'

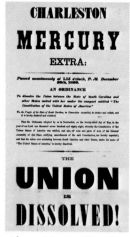

stars and then descend, gaining speed. A capital shot, they observed. It fell directly into the empty parade ground in the center of the fort and exploded.

That first shot was followed by a storm of fire as 30 guns and 17 mortars opened up from Rebel batteries around the harbor. The Federals in Sumter decided the show was getting less entertaining and retired to the bombproofs. As the shells burst deafeningly around and inside the fort, the men had a grim breakfast of boiled pork – the only food left. After reveille the Union guns were manned; at about 7:30 Doubleday fired the first answering round.

Short of ammunition and realizing the enemy fire on the parapets was severe, Major Anderson abandoned the guns on that level; Federal answering fire proceeded from guns on the casements, effecting little damage to the well-armored batteries of the Rebels, one of them a floating ironclad battery that bounded away Federal shot like so many peas.

Around one in the afternoon three ships hove into view: Federal relief vessels that Anderson had been told to expect. The garrison cheered but soon

Above: News of South Carolina's secession.
Left: The capture of Fort Sumter.

have the honor to notify you that we will open the fire . . . in one hour from this time.' Sumter's commander notified Captain Abner Doubleday (later to become incorrectly known as the founder of modern baseball) that the attack would begin at first light and that to conserve ammunition, fire should not be returned until broad daylight. After giving his final notice to Major Anderson, General Beauregard sent firing orders to Captain G S James in Fort Johnson, on James Island. Captain James offered a friend the 'honor' of discharging the opening shot; the friend, agitated, replied, 'I could not fire the first gun of the war.' At 4:30 AM, 12 April, Captain James himself pulled the lanyard.

The defenders saw the flash of the mortar, watched the burning fuse of the shell mount into the

Above: Union artillery, 1861.
Far left: Subsequent warfare like that between the French (pictured here) and the Prussians was influenced by Civil War tactics.
Left: Fort Sumter after the capture.

Opposite: Abraham Lincoln (1809-1865). His election to the presidency made it inevitable that the South would secede from the Union, not because he opposed slavery as an institution where it already existed, but because he opposed its extension into new territories.

saw the ships turn back in the face of steady enemy fire. The Federals broke off at dusk, having used only six cannons during the day. No one had yet been killed or injured on either side and the damage to the fort was slight – only a few fires, easily contained. All during the night Confederate shells continued to fall into the fort; few could sleep, and all were anxious about the coming day. Would the enemy attack? Would reinforcements arrive?

During that first day's shelling General Beauregard had noticed the flames in Sumter. They were created by the Rebel batteries' hot shot – cannon-balls heated red-hot before firing. Beauregard decided to use more of these, and in the next day's action the hot shot had a devastating effect on the fort. By midmorning of 13 April the wooden barracks, supposedly fireproof, were in flames, and the fire was moving ominously close to the magazine. Major Anderson detailed a number of men to keep the flames away from the powder, but directed that shooting should continue – one shot every five minutes, no more than token fire.

During the action a Union cannoneer, attempting to load his piece, discovered a face peering into the embrasure. This proved to be a Confederate emissary, ex-Senator Wigfall of Texas, who earnestly pleaded to be allowed in before he was killed by his own side's fire. Noticing he carried a white handkerchief on a sword, the cannoneer hauled the intruder in. Wigfall had come to offer surrender terms. After some confused negotiations, these were agreed to by Major Anderson. Fort Sumter, indefensible at the outset, had endured 34 hours of bombardment and some 4000 shells: there was clearly little point in continued resistance. And there were still no casualties on either side.

It was agreed that the Federals would evacuate the fort on 14 April, and that they might salute their flag with 100 guns before leaving. During this salute some sparks from the smoldering fires accidentally ignited a cannon cartridge as it was being loaded; the resulting explosion killed Private Daniel Hough instantly and seriously wounded five others, one of whom died. In this pointless accident fell the first soldiers of the war.

Below: Fort Sumter would be hotly contested throughout the war, primarily as a symbolic rather than a strategic objective.
Right: The outer wall commanding Charleston Harbor.

After their salute the Federals marched out, banners flying, the band playing 'Yankee Doodle,' and sailed off on the steamer *Baltic* to a heroes'

welcome in New York. Confederate forces marched into the fort with equal ceremony. To observers and participants alike it had all seemed a rather dashing and gentlemanly affair, on the whole, and not a particularly dangerous one; more like a grand fireworks show. Maybe that's how it will be, many Southerners thought: we shell them a little and they go away. Maybe it would all be this easy.

But the South did not yet know the resolve of Abraham Lincoln. On 15 April the President declared a state of 'insurrection' and called for 75,000 volunteers to join the regular army in suppressing it. Northern States were immediately supportive, Border States resistant. On 19 April Lincoln declared a blockade of all Confederate ports. In the wake of Sumter four more states seceded – Virginia, Arkansas, Tennessee and North Carolina – but the Border States – Delaware, Maryland, Kentucky and Missouri – stayed loyal. Six days after Sumter fell, US Army General Robert E Lee declined an offer to command Union forces, resigned his commission and proclaimed his duty to defend his home state of Virginia. Sumter was destined to stay in Southern hands until the very end, despite massive Union shelling. To both sides, it would remain a powerful symbol of victory and of defiance.

Thus came the opening act of the war. Everywhere citizens rallied to the colors, galvanized by romantic visions of a noble cause, of heroic battle. But a few, above all Abraham Lincoln, already understood that the coming conflict would be no glorious game but rather a tragedy of immeasurable magnitude.

Above: William Seward, Lincoln's Secretary of State. *Left:* Jefferson Davis, President of the Confederacy.

The First Battle of Bull Run, Manassas, Virginia, 21 July 1861. This Confederate victory (called First Manassas by Southerners) proved to the North that the war had begun in earnest.

CHAPTER TWO
SHILOH
GRANT STRIKES BACK

Opposite: General Ulysses S Grant, whose unimposing appearance belied his performance at the head of his armies. *Below:* General Ambrose Burnside's Brigade at the First Battle of Bull Run. *Bottom:* CSA Light Guards at Fort Sumter, 1861.

IN APRIL OF 1862 THE war was a year old, and the original optimistic hopes on both sides for a short conflict, resolved in one or two decisive battles, were fading. After the fall of Fort Sumter, Lincoln had called for three-month volunteers to put down the rebellion. That was expected to be time enough. But the initial major battle of the war, the First Bull Run (Virginia) in July 1861, had been a humiliation for the Union, as had the action at Ball's Bluff, Virginia, in October.

It began to be clear that in order to defeat the South, the North had to invade and occupy it. If the North could be said at this stage to have a strategy to achieve that gargantuan task, it was to split the Confederacy on a north-south line along the Mississippi River, then east-west somewhere through the middle of the South; then it would deal with the fragments. To achieve the north-south sundering, Federal forces early in 1862 began moving south into Rebel territory from Kentucky, along the Cumberland and Tennessee Rivers.

The district commander of these forces was an up-and-coming Union general named Ulysses S Grant. In February 1862 Grant had leaped from utter obscurity into national prominence with his dramatic campaigns to capture Forts Henry and Donelson. His surrender note to the latter – 'No terms except for immediate and unconditional surrender can be accepted' – had earned him the nickname 'Unconditional Surrender' Grant.

But no one really knew yet what Grant was capable of. He was an unkempt and not particularly soldierly looking man whose gait was a sort of controlled stumble. His habitual expression was once

Top: The Battle of Shiloh, Tennessee, 6 April 1862.
Above: Abolitionist John Brown, who was executed for his prewar raid on the Federal arsenal at Harper's Ferry, Virginia.

described in the words 'He looked as if he had decided to drive his head through a brick wall and was about to do it.' There was talk, perhaps more than rumor, about his past – failures in business, a near-court-martial in his first military command some years before and a fondness for the bottle abnormal even for an officer. And after his recent victories Grant had somehow displeased his superiors enough to get himself relieved of command and virtually under arrest for a week. Only when mounted did Grant seem to come into his own, to look like a leader: he was a superb horseman. All in all, though, he was no one's image of a great commander.

When Grant got back his district command on 13 March, he found his army on the Tennessee River, part at the small town of Savannah, Tennessee, and part nine miles above, on the western bank of the river near Pittsburg Landing, Tennessee. His plan was to concentrate these forces, called the Union Army of the Mississippi, with those of General Don Carlos Buell's Army of the Ohio; the latter were ordered to move southwest from Nashville. When finally combined, the two armies were to move on

Corinth, Mississippi, an important Confederate rail center (all these towns were near the conjoined corners of Tennessee, Mississippi and Alabama). Buell began promptly to move his forces, but then was held up for ten days by floods.

Grant did know there were enemy forces near his camps and a large Rebel force in Corinth. He did not know, however, that they were preparing an offensive designed to smash his army before Buell could reach him. (As was often the case during the war, Southern intelligence-gathering was more accurate than that of the North.) For the purpose of dealing with Grant's forces, General P G T Beauregard, the hero of Sumter and Bull Run, had assembled in Corinth a new Confederate Army of 40,000 men, consisting of corps under Generals Leonidas Polk, Braxton Bragg, William J Hardee, and John C Breckenridge. In overall command of this new Confederate Army of the Mississippi was General Albert Sidney Johnston, who was considered among the greatest hopes of the Southern cause.

Johnston developed a bold offensive strategy, overruling Beauregard's insistence on a defensive approach. According to the plan, the Confederate

Army was to move out of Corinth, envelop the Union left flank by the river – thus cutting off reinforcements from Buell in the east – and push the Federals back to Owl Creek to the northeast, thereby forcing a surrender.

On 6 April Grant had six divisions – those of John A McClernand, William H Wallace, Lew Wallace (later the writer of *Ben Hur*), Steven A Hurlbut, William Tecumseh Sherman and Benjamin M Prentiss – encamped on the west side of the Tennessee River in the vicinity of Pittsburg Landing and the little log meetinghouse called Shiloh Church. A considerable portion of these 33,000 troops were quite green; indeed, many scarcely knew how to load their rifles, and some of the officers were little more experienced.

Though there had been continuous skirmishing along his front for some days, Grant wrote his superior Halleck on 5 April, 'I scarcely have the faintest idea of an attack . . . being made on us.' Grant's close associate Sherman concurred with this supposition: they reasoned that Corinth was a good defensive position and the Confederates would not venture out of it. The Union camps were therefore chosen for their comfort rather than for their defensive strength; guarding was desultory, and there were no entrenchments. The soldiers themselves, however, seemed to suspect more than their officers that the skirmishes were significant, that something big was coming.

On the morning of 6 April Grant confidently left his camp well before dawn to have breakfast in Savannah and meet with Buell, who had arrived there the day before. Grant was on crutches, lamed by a riding accident. Most of his troops were beginning a normal day, having a leisurely breakfast and polishing up for the usual Sunday inspection

Then, still before dawn, the Rebel attack swarmed into the Union camps with overpowering suddenness and strength. Beauregard later wrote of the onset of the battle:

About 5 AM the Confederate lines were set in motion. The first collision was in the quarter of Gladden's brigade, on our right, and with a battalion of five companies of the 21st [actually the 25th] Missouri of Prentiss's division dispatched well to the front by General Prentiss, of his own motion, as early as 3 AM. But for this incident, due solely to the intelligent, soldierly forethought of an officer not trained to the business of war, the whole Federal front would have been struck wholly unawares, for nowhere else had such

Top: Ulysses S Grant in the field.
Above: Union ships of the Port Royal expedition scatter the Confederate garrison at Fort Walker, South Carolina, in November 1861.
Left: Fighting in the woods around Shiloh Church at Pittsburg Landing, Tennessee, where inexperienced Union troops suffered heavy losses.

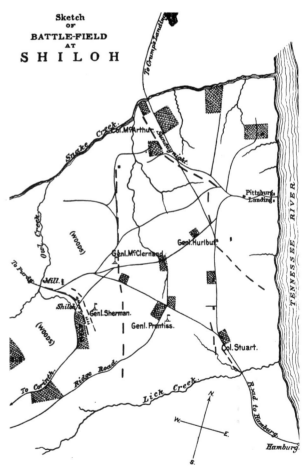

Sketch
OF
BATTLE-FIELD
AT
SHILOH

Top: The Confederate
defeat at Pea Ridge,
Arkansas, in the Trans-
Mississippi Theater (6-8
March 1862).
Above: Union troops
land at Fort Walker.
Right: The battlefield at
Shiloh.

prudence been shown. Exactly at 6 AM Prentiss's
whole division was under fire, and the battle of
Shiloh began in earnest.

Companies of the 16th Wisconsin and 21st Missouri were sent to reinforce the slim Union forces in
the front, but these were soon driven back. The
majority of the 25th Missouri (on the left middle of
the Union lines) were standing at rest in their camp
when they were astonished to see a huge body of
Confederates, line after line, unpreceded by skirmishers, coming down a slope toward them within
easy range. (A thin line of skirmishers was almost
invariably used to screen the main force and draw
out the enemy.) Both sides simply stood and fired
away, with devastating effect – at this point in the
war, many considered it cowardly to dig a hole or
even to take cover.

Meanwhile, at six o'clock that morning, Hilde-
brand's hastily formed brigade of Sherman's division, on the right of the Union lines, received the
full force of the Confederate attack. Green troops of

the 53rd Ohio immediately broke and ran, followed
by two other regiments. The rest of Sherman's
division fell back from their camps after some resistance, and by eight in the morning Prentiss's
whole division had done likewise, pursued through
their camps and across a ravine. It seemed as if a
total Union rout were imminent.

About that same hour, Confederate General
Johnston's designs on the left flank of the Federal
army – the original focal point of his strategy of
envelopment – began to take shape. On the extreme

Union left was a small brigade of Sherman's division, without artillery, led by Colonel David Stuart. His small force met a strong charge by the Rebels and, after some initial panic, was formed into line and mounted a furious resistance some 500 yards behind their original position. This Union stand, coming as it did after a frightened stampede, was so determined that it convinced the enemy it must be a trap: as one Rebel officer observed, 'No such little body of men could ever stand up and fight like that without something back of them.' A Union soldier, describing later the experience of the defenders, gives a good insight into the feelings of men in battle: 'The infantry poured such a shower of lead in upon us as rapidly to reduce our ranks to half the original number. Only the excitement of battle could sustain a man in the midst of such carnage. As man after man was shot down or mutilated, a feeling of perfect horror came over me at times, and I berated the powers which placed us in such a position.' Stuart's brigade would hold on until after two o'clock that afternoon, withdrawing only when its ammunition was exhausted. The wary Confederates, still suspecting a trap and not realizing how small a force had stayed them, did not immediately press their advantage.

By midmorning the fighting was furious all along the line. The battle clearly had the appearance of a major Confederate victory. Most of the Union forces had pulled back from their camps with heavy losses. There was a serious gap in the center of the Federal line, and hordes of Union stragglers were collecting along the river to the rear. The raw volunteers of the Northern armies had experienced their baptism of fire, seen all war's horrors for the first time – men everywhere in every state of pain and mutilation, wounded horses running screaming with their entrails dragging in the dust, the bone-chilling screech of the Rebel yell as attack after attack pushed the defenders back, the incredible din of battle as the fire of countless cannons and rifles

Below: General Grant's charge at Shiloh.
Bottom: Grant's forces fighting for Fort Donelson, Tennessee, before the Battle of Shiloh.

blended with screams into one continuous and apocalyptic roar. In the face of this horror and chaos, so utterly different from the romantic notions of battle entertained by most young soldiers, it is not surprising that many, officers as well as men, broke and ran; it is surprising rather that the majority stood and fought – sometimes with extraordinary tenacity.

It is useful to understand that the progress of battle in a history book is very different from the perspective of the commander in the field. Battlefield communications during the Civil War were always shaky, and this early phase of the war lacked even the primitive telegraph equipment and balloons of later engagements. Dispatches were sent on foot or on horseback, and what field commanders sent to their superiors was limited to their own narrow view of the battle – thus superiors often received contradictory messages from various parts of the field. Visual information was limited by the presence of woods and hills, and also by the thick blanket of smoke that invariably covered the battlefield (smokeless powder was not in use during the war). Commanding officers often had to rely on their ears to deduce the progress of battle: an experienced soldier could hear the size of forces, hear attacks, hear defeat, hear victory. And, conversely, a clever commander could arrange for the enemy to hear armies and attacks that were not really there (this technique proved vital to the usually outnumbered Confederate Army in later campaigns such as Yorktown and the Seven Days).

Things were indeed going well enough for the Confederacy on the morning of 6 April, but not so well as they seemed to the Rebels. Johnston's attack was in fact poorly organized: his units had intermingled, the commands becoming confused; men were thrown into attack by columns as they arrived on the roads, and no reserves were left at all; the main thrust of Johnston's original attack plan, the left of the Union line, had bogged down. Instead of the intended envelopment, there was a disorderly advance all along the front.

Furthermore, Union forces were withdrawing not in disarray but rather in good order, the stragglers notwithstanding. Having heard the onset of hostilities that morning, Grant rushed to Pittsburg Landing from Savannah, arriving about eight o'clock. Not having had time to see Buell in Savannah, Grant sent a note to hurry him along. Lew Wallace was ordered to rush his 5000 troops south from Crump's Landing (confusion about the orders delayed Wallace until after dark). Guards were placed in the rear to stop stragglers at gunpoint. Hearing that General 'Bull' Nelson's division, the closest part of Buell's army, had arrived at Savannah, Grant ordered them to move to the east bank of the Tennessee opposite Pittsburg Landing. Determined Federal resistance remained on the left (Stuart) and also in a densely wooded area on the left center, dubbed by the Confederate attackers 'The Hornet's Nest.' Grant asked Prentiss to hold the Hornet's Nest, the key to the middle of his line, at all costs. As the battle progressed, Grant moved from point to point within his lines, gathering firsthand information and encouraging commanders and troops.

At half past two in the afternoon came a crushing blow both to Southern fortunes in the battle and to

An early Civil War camp, one of the hundreds that would become a feature of the Southern landscape in years to come.

hopes for the Confederate cause itself. General Johnston had ridden over to the right of his lines to deal with what was intended as his main thrust, on the Federal left. He found his men still bogged down in the face of galling Union fire. Johnston ordered a charge and personally led his men in pushing the Federals back some three-quarters of a mile. While dressing their lines in the new position, the Confederates found themselved subject to enfilade fire from the left. Johnston had just ordered one regiment to wheel and meet this fire when he was struck by a stray shot and sagged on his horse. I G Harris, the Governor of Tennessee, righted the general and led his horse behind the lines. Johnston had previously dispatched his chief surgeon to the rear, to deal with Federal wounded. This act of charity probably cost him his life. The shot had cut an artery, but the wound could easily have been treated had the surgeon been available. Without help, Johnston bled to death in a few minutes. The South thereby lost one of its greatest generals and the Confederate attack began to lose momentum. Beauregard, who had strenuously opposed the offensive tactic and was also quite ill at the time, was now in command of the Southern forces.

But the Confederate advance by no means came to an immediate halt. The Federal left was at length pushed back almost to Pittsburg Landing, threatening the arrival of Buell's reinforcements as Johnston had intended. On the Union left center, the Hornet's Nest held on with divisions of Hurlbut and W H L Wallace, along with the remnants of Prentiss's division. The Federal position here was formidable, posted in a dense thicket on the crest of

Above: 'Kill the Yanks — Shoot Them!' by Samuel J Reader.
Left: Union forces launch a successful charge at the Battle of Shiloh.

President Abraham Lincoln visits his generals in the field in the early days of the war.

a hill. Southern attackers had to cross an open field through a murderous crossfire from rifles in the front and batteries on their flanks. One of Prentiss's artillery officers would describe the fighting in this area:

Quickly came the orders sharp and clear: 'Shrapnel,' 'Two seconds,' 'One second,' 'Canister.' Then, as the enemy made preparation for their final dash, 'double canister' was ordered delivered with such rapidity that the separate discharges were blended into one continuous roar. . . . Again and again, through long and trying hours, this dance of death went on at frequent intervals from nine in the morning until four in the afternoon.

In all, the Rebels mounted 11 unsuccessful charges on the Hornet's Nest. But at length the Federal defenders grew exhausted, and the retreat of their own forces around them slowly exposed their flanks. Finally, Confederate General Ruggles massed 62 cannon on the position and encircled it.

Federal General W H L Wallace was killed leading his division to safety out of the area. At half past five in the afternoon General Prentiss and 2200 men surrendered after some eight hours of fighting.

But the Federal's stand in the Hornet's Nest had been more than empty heroics. The number of men and the time it took to take the position had slowed the whole Confederate thrust. It took yet more valuable time to disarm the Federal prisoners, gather them and send them to the rear, where other Southern soldiers, thinking the bulk of the Federal Army had been taken, left their positions to go peer curiously at the 'captured Yanks.'

It was therefore some time before Confederate forces were gathered again for what was intended to be the decisive move on the Union Army. At Pittsburg Landing the Federals had fallen back as far as the ground permitted; one more strong Rebel push would send them into the river. At that most critical moment, artillery came to the rescue of the North. Grant's artillery chief, Colonel J D Webster, opened up from a battery on high ground near the landing; the Union iron-clad gunboats *Lexington* and *Tyler*, just arrived from Savannah, opened up with long-range 64-pounders on the Rebel positions. In the face of this bombardment, the enemy advance ground to a halt. Soon came yet another moment to cheer the Federals: troops of Nelson's division of Buell's army, the desperately awaited reinforcements, were seen gathering on the east shore. In short order they were being ferried across the Tennessee.

At about six that evening, just before a final Rebel attack was to be made on Pittsburg Landing, Beauregard suspended operations, to the dismay of several of his commanders. He did so partly because night was coming, partly because he was ignorant of Buell's impending arrival. His intelligence reported that Buell could not be expected to arrive in time to aid Grant, and therefore the Southerners could take time to rest and regroup.

It cannot be said with certainty that a final Confederate attack on the landing would have succeeded, though it would have had a good chance to do so on that evening of 6 April. It can be said, however, that Beauregard's decision to end the fighting at that point doomed the South's last chance to win the battle. Union commanders began forming stragglers and retreating units into a strong line that by nightfall stretched in an arc curving generally west-northwest from Pittsburg Landing. Reinforcements began pouring in from Buell in the east and from Lew Wallace in the north.

But between the contending forces, it was the Confederates who that night assumed they had won. Back in the captured Union camps, the Rebels celebrated with the enemy's provisions and liquor, enjoying the shelter of the tents when a storm blew in; Union troops had to bivouac outside in the torrential rain. True, the Rebels were harried by the Union gunboats, which continued to shell their positons all night, but neither that nor the rain could dampen the Southerners' sense of impending victory.

It was not yet generally known to the enemy that U S Grant was not in the habit of giving up, whatever the circumstances. During that wet and miserable night Grant hobbled about, kept awake by the pain of his riding injury and sickened by the suffering of his wounded men. Nonetheless, he thought coolly and clearly. He saw that the next day's victory would go to whoever attacked first, and made his plans accordingly. All night, while the Confederates were celebrating, Buell's men were being transported across the Tennessee – divisions led by Crittenden, McCook and Nelson, totaling 25,000 men, all of them fresh. Lew Wallace's division of 5000 finally arrived after dark. This was entirely unknown to Beauregard, who expected the imminent arrival of 20,000 reinforcements under General Van Dorn, moving up from Arkansas.

On 7 April, at seven-thirty in the morning, Grant's supposedly beaten Federals unleashed a well-co-ordinated counterattack on both enemy flanks, led by Lew Wallace on the Union right and Nelson, of Buell's army, on the left. Wallace began with his artillery, dueling with the enemy cannon, and sent his soldiers across a ravine onto the Southern flank; the enemy hastily withdrew with their own guns. Nelson pressed forward with equal success on the left. By 10:30 the fighting was general all along the line, and the Federals had regained much of the ground lost the previous day.

A Southern offensive developed around a peach orchard on the Union right; the Federals, having outrun their artillery, gave way for a time. At length Union artillery was moved up and General Buell directed the assault; after a seesaw contest the Rebel lines were again driven away. By early afternoon the Confederate right had been pushed back and the Federals had reoccupied their original camps, recapturing weapons and materiel they had abandoned the day before. Beauregard mounted a strong resistance in front of the crossroads by Shiloh Church, now his headquarters; the roads there were Van Dorn's best route to reinforce Beauregard, and also the best route on which to retreat, if it came to that. Beauregard had only 20,000 men left fighting. Without Van Dorn, he saw that it would indeed

An 1863 engraving of Union military strategist and general Henry Halleck.

come to retreat. He held onto the crossroads grimly for a time; the insignificant meetinghouse became the focal point of the battle that would bear its name.

By two-thirty that afternoon Beauregard had learned that Van Dorn had been halted by the swollen Mississippi. The Federals were pushing back his forces all along the line, casualties were mounting and straggling was becoming uncontrollable – troops fell out by the hundreds and streamed to the rear. There was only one option left: Beauregard issued orders to retreat. The Confederates withdrew toward Corinth in good order, the retreat covered by infantry and artillery under General Nathan Bedford Forrest. At three o'clock Grant personally directed a last Union charge along the road to Corinth. By five o'clock, the Rebels had retired from the field.

The Federals sank into their recaptured camps and did not pursue. It is possible that pursuit might have captured or wiped out Beauregard's whole army, but throughout the war it was to remain true that, given the mobile character of the fighting, its furious charges and countercharges, armies were ordinarily too exhausted after battle to mount effective pursuit. Federal pursuit of Beauregard – begun some days later by the inept General Halleck, who took command from Grant after the battle – was too little and too late. It took Halleck three weeks to cover the 31 miles to Corinth, and when he got there Beauregard's army was gone.

In the ensuing days both sides claimed victory, and in fact, Union casualties were greater. But it was unquestionably a Union victory, if an incomplete one. The South had begun with a tactical surprise – much disputed by Grant in his memoirs, but a sur-prise all the same – and had fought gallantly and with great initial effect. But the Rebel attack had been poorly co-ordinated and overextended; those facts, combined with the disaster of Johnston's death, had allowed the Federals to regroup and finally to take the initiative. As is usually the case, the side with the initiative gained the victory.

In those two days at Shiloh the North gained a great deal more than a simple victory. They sustained an invasion deep into enemy territory, preparing the way for eventual domination of the Mississippi and a vertical split of the Confederacy. But these achievements lay in the future. The limited perspective at the end of the battle saw only an almost accidental victory: generalship on both sides had been poor. It was therefore largely a 'soldiers' battle,' one carried on and finally won by the pluck and valor of individuals. As a later commentator observed, 'At Shiloh there had been . . . no relation of one command to another; no defined front or known rear except an impassable river. There was no common directing head or superior officer beyond the rank of division commander on the firing line. There was nothing to give cohesion to the whole. . . . It was a private soldiers' battle, fiercely fought by unskilled, uninstructed and inexperienced volunteers, supported by the indomitable energy, desperate courage and marvelous staying qualities of the rank and file.'

In short, the generals on both sides that day still had lessons to learn on the art of war. Many of those lessons were about to be taught, to the North's despair, by Lee and Jackson.

Shiloh is regarded as one of the three largest, most desperate and most important battles of the war (the other two usually mentioned are Antietam and

Union forces at Camp Griffin, Virginia, in 1861

Left: Thaddeus S C Lowe demonstrates the use of a hot-air balloon for reconnaissance purposes to Union troops.

Above: Confederate General Albert Sidney Johnston, a leader of great promise who was killed in action at Shiloh.

Gettysburg). It was the first known battle in the Western Hemisphere to involve over 100,000 men. Casualties were appalling on both sides: of around 62,682 Union effectives (by the second day), 1754 were killed, 8408 wounded and 2885 missing, for a total of 13,047 casualties; of the South's 40,335 effectives, 1723 were killed, 8012 wounded, 959 missing, for a total of 10,694.

Both by the magnitude of its losses and by its inconclusiveness, Shiloh changed the nature and perception of the war. Grant himself saw this and later wrote:

Up to the battle of Shiloh, I, as well as thousands of other citizens, believed that the rebellion . . . would collapse suddenly and soon if a decisive victory could be gained over any of its armies. Henry and Donelson were such victories. Clarksville and Nashville, Tennessee . . . also fell into our hands. The Tennessee and Cumberland rivers were secured. But when Confederate armies were collected which not only attempted to hold a line farther south . . ., but assumed the offensive, and made such a gallant effort to regain what had been lost, then indeed I gave up all idea of saving the Union except by complete conquest.

In short, Grant began to understand after Shiloh that a phenomenon was evolving – what later generations would call Total War: war waged by the whole population and resources of one people upon the whole population and resources of another.

Beauregard's defeat was to damage his prestige for some time during the war. As for Grant, he had been surprised, and the brilliance of his holding on and striking back did not erase that fact. But Lincoln, seeing things clearly from distant Washington, was soon to reply to demands for Grant's dismissal with eloquent simplicity: 'I can't spare this man. He fights.'

The Battle of Antietam, 17 September 1862. General George B McClellan leads the Army of the Potomac against Robert E Lee's forces along Antietam Creek.

THE FORTUNES OF THE Eastern Theater during the war were destined to lie largely in the hands of two legendary armies, which for three years warily circled, paused and then mauled one another with unbridled violence. In the summer of 1862 these armies – the Federal Army of the Potomac and the Confederate Army of Northern Virginia – were young and ambitious: each set out with high hopes on a campaign of invasion intended to turn the tide of the war. The escalating series of clashes that resulted, climaxing in the devastating Battle of Antietam, was to bring both armies to a quick and agonizing maturity.

At the beginning of 1862, neither of these armies was yet the historic entity it was soon to become. The Army of Northern Virginia was called the Confederate Army of the Potomac; its commander was General Joseph E Johnston, leader of victorious Southern forces in the First Bull Run.

Commanding the Army of the Potomac was General George B McClellan. This short and energetic man was to create a great army, but in the end he would not be the one to lead it to victory. After a series of minor successes in Virginia and Kentucky the 34-year-old McClellan was brought to Washington and, during the winter of 1861-62, given all the resources of the North to create his army. This he did brilliantly, bringing to the task a remarkable gift for organization and detail. He loved his army and they loved him, dubbing him affectionately 'Little

Right: General George B McClellan, creator of the Army of the Potomac, named Union General-in-Chief in December 1861.
Below: The bustling Wall Street Ferry in New York City, commercial capital of the North.

Left: Grapevine bridge
on the Chickahominy
River, 18 June 1862.
Below: Confederate
General Joseph E
Johnston, who fought
throughout the war.

Mac' and 'The Young Napoleon.' In December
McClellan was named general-in-chief of Union
Armies, succeeding superannuated General Win-
field Scott.

But the thoroughness and attention to detail that
made McClellan a great builder of armies, as well as
the very affection he felt for his men, were to prove
his greatest faults on the battlefield: his elaborate
caution and his protective attitude toward the army
made him ponderous and indecisive in action (and
his opponent Robert E Lee had the opposite
qualities). As someone later wrote of McClellan:
'Though no commander ever had the love of his
soldiers more, or tried more to spare their lives, [he]
never realized the metal that was in his grand Army
of the Potomac.'

In the first months of 1862, General Joseph E
Johnston's Confederate Army lay at Centreville,
Virginia, only 30 miles from Washington. McClel-
lan's army was ready to move against this enemy as
spring approached, but McClellan himself was not.
With increasing impatience Lincoln prodded
McClellan, finally issuing on 22 February General
War Order No 1, mandating a movement against
the enemy. McClellan stalled and stalled, fretting
over his arrangements and cautioned by his chief of
intelligence, Alan Pinkerton, that Confederates in
Virginia vastly outnumbered Federal forces.
(Pinkerton's exaggerated estimates of enemy
strength were disastrous to the Union war effort
during most of 1862.)

General Robert E Lee, who would end the war as Commander-in-Chief of Confederate Armies – a sadly reduced assemblage by 1865.

Lincoln wanted the Army of the Potomac to move by land and push Johnston away, staying between the enemy and Washington. McClellan produced a plan to move against the Confederate capital at Richmond by water from the south; he reasoned rightly that Washington's defenses were adequate to any eventuality and that Johnston would be obliged to follow any Federal movement. When Johnston withdrew southwest to Culpeper, Virginia, Lincoln, still concerned about Washington's vulnerability, reluctantly consented to McClellan's plan. However, to allow McClellan to concentrate on the campaign, and also because of his justifiable worries about his general, Lincoln relieved McClellan as overall Union commander and took on those duties himself. (Until he found the general he was looking for, Lincoln would involve himself in military operations, and in fact his ideas of strategy were often better than those of his generals – but he lacked the means to implement his ideas.)

By 5 April 1862 McClellan had landed 121,500 men at Fort Monroe, on the toe of the peninsula between the James and York Rivers, some 70 miles from Richmond. The Peninsular Campaign was under way at last; the slogan of the day was 'On to Richmond!'

McClellan was expecting to be reinforced by the corps of Generals McDowell and Banks, moving over from their positions in Virginia's Shenandoah Valley. But during the landing word came from Lincoln that due to dangerous movements by Stonewall Jackson in the Valley that might eventually threaten Washington, McDowell and Banks must stay where they were. Lincoln's letter concluded impatiently, '*But you must act.*'

Furious at losing the two corps, and not fooled by Jackson's diversion, McClellan began a steady stream of letters to Washington demanding reinforcements. Reluctantly, he started moving his army up the peninsula toward Richmond, but stopped almost immediately in front of Confederate defenses that stretched from Yorktown across the peninsula. These defenses were actually manned by only 15,000 Southerners, but McClellan, advised by Pinkerton that enemy forces were formidable, spent a month mounting an elaborate siege of Yorktown – which could easily have been taken by assault in one day. The Confederate commander at Yorktown, General John B Magruder, was an amateur actor; he produced a fine show for the Yankees, marching the same regiments in and out of various positions to convince his enemy that there were fearsome defenses. McClellan was only too ready to swallow the deception; he called Magruder's thin line 'one of the most extensive known to modern times.'

The Confederate command was both astonished and delighted at McClellan's siege – it gave them all the time they needed to prepare their resistance. The plans were formulated by Robert E Lee, at that time serving as military advisor to Confederate

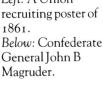

Left: A Union recruiting poster of 1861.
Below: Confederate General John B Magruder.

President Jefferson Davis. During April Johnston amassed 60,000 men on McClellan's front, successfully tying up 112,000 Federals while defenses were constructed around Richmond. These defenses completed, Johnston pulled back from Yorktown to Richmond on 3 May. Next day McClellan finally unleashed his mighty attack. There were precious few enemy around to resist it. The Federals then began inching again up the peninsula, beset by an unusually rainy spring and virtually impassable roads. Lincoln observed wearily to his friends that McClellan was infected with 'the slows.'

Meanwhile, in the Shenandoah Valley of Vir-

Above: The bayonet charge of the New York 9th Hawkins' Zouaves at Roanoke Island in the Western Theater, 1862. Bayonet fighting was uncommon in the Civil War.

Above: A
contemporary artist's
view of the Shenandoah
Valley Campaign of
1862.
Opposite: President
Lincoln confers with
General McClellan in
the field at Antietam.

ginia, the main geographic avenue between North
and South, one of the most remarkable campaigns in
military history was throwing the entire Federal war
effort into confusion. Its leader was a strange, soft-
spoken and compulsively religious man named
Thomas J Jackson, known to the entire country after
the First Bull Run as 'Stonewall.' Mysterious and
unco-operative to both superiors and subordinates
(some of whom questioned his sanity), a martinet to
his men (he nearly killed them himself with incessant marching), he was to become the irreplaceable
partner of Lee. To history, he is a military genius of
the first rank: the Shenandoah Valley Campaign of
spring and summer 1862 was his first and perhaps
greatest masterpiece.

Jackson was ordered by Lee to make a 'strategic
diversion' in the Shenandoah, to keep McDowell
and Banks from reinforcing McClellan – a com-
bination Lee and Johnston well knew would be fatal.
On 23 March Jackson met Banks at Kernstown, and
there the Confederates suffered a repulse. But
Kernstown might just as well have been a Southern
victory: the attack threw Washington into a panic;
Rebel forces were expected momentarily at the gates
of the city. Lincoln ordered Banks and McDowell,
as well as General Frémont, to stay in the Valley to
deal with Jackson rather than reinforcing the Army
of the Potomac. This single decision, which made

McClellan even more cautious in approaching
Richmond, may have served to prolong the war for
three years.

Jackson at that time had only 10,000 men, but
was soon reinforced by 7000 under General Richard
S Ewell. While the Union opposition mobilized
awkwardly, with no unity of command, Jackson
began his Valley Campaign in earnest in April.
Leaving Ewell at Swift Run Gap to hold Banks,
Jackson and his division left secretly, marched south
to Port Republic, crossed the mountains, trained
across to Staunton (his men boarding dejectedly,
supposing they were retiring to Richmond) and
marched to defeat the Federals (8 May) at the town
of McDowell, on the western side of the Valley.
Jackson's fast-marching soldiers began to be called
admiringly the 'foot cavalry.'

After chasing the Federals from McDowell, Jackson rushed northeast to Harrisonburg; there he
screened his movements with cavalry to deceive
Banks while going east across the mountains to join
Ewell. These combined forces descended suddenly
on 1000 Federals at Front Royal (23 May), wiping
out the detachment. Marching day and night, the
foot cavalry moved to meet Banks at Winchester;
defeating him there on 25 May, Jackson chased
Banks's forces back to the Potomac.

By 29 May Jackson was concentrating near the

Federal garrison at Harper's Ferry, at the northern end of the Shenandoah. Banks, Frémont and McDowell were converging around him. But Jackson eluded them all and by 1 June had escaped with 15,000 troops, 2000 prisoners and a seven-mile-long double wagon train of captured munitions and booty. The Federals pursued as best they could. On 7 June Jackson found himself between two enemy columns totaling 20,000 men. He struck one column (at Cross Keys), then the other (at Port Republic) on 8-9 June, defeated both, and the Federals withdrew. The Confederates with their booty then rushed to join Johnston in resisting McClellan on the peninsula.

It had been an astonishing campaign. In 11 weeks Jackson and his men had marched 630 miles in mountainous country, fought numerous skirmishes and four major battles, tied up three Federal armies totaling 62,000 men, inflicted 7000 casualties and captured enormous quantities of materiel plus 3000 prisoners. All this was accomplished with a maximum strength of 17,000 men – usually less – and with casualties of some 3100. Jackson had thrown the Northern war effort into confusion – they never suspected how few his numbers were, never knew where he would strike next. Jackson once observed, 'always mystify, mislead, and surprise the enemy if possible.' The Shenandoah Valley Campaign amply demonstrated that maxim.

Above: Confederate Cavalry General Joseph O Shelby.
Right: General J E B ('Jeb') Stuart, who became a Civil War legend as a dashing cavalry commander.
Below: The Battle of Fair Oaks, Virginia, 31 May 1862.

While Jackson was careering around the Shenandoah, McClellan was still inching warily up the peninsula. By May the Army of the Potomac had reached and straddled the Chickahominy River, very near to Richmond. Confederate General Johnston, finding Keyes's X Corps isolated south of the river, decided to attack him in the hope of destroying the whole army. In the resulting battle of Fair Oaks (1 June) the Rebel offensive was poorly coordinated; in the resulting Federal repulse of the attack, Johnston was seriously wounded.

But as with Jackson's defeat at Kernstown, this Federal victory was to benefit the South unexpectedly: Johnston's replacement was General Robert E Lee, who took command at the age of 55 in early June, immediately renaming his forces the Army of Northern Virginia.

Lee's life and reputation are paradoxical – honored in history as one of the greatest of all Americans, he was a primary leader of a rebellion that aimed to destroy the Union; privately a quiet and religious man, in battle he was one of the most aggressive generals of all time. So reserved and courtly was Lee that at first his men dubbed him 'Granny.' But it took very little time for his prowess to become known to his own soldiers, who virtually deified him. Even the Union Army counted on Lee to be the most dangerous man in the field.

Beyond his own daring and innovative tactical skills, Lee commanded an outstanding group of subordinates: the incomparable Jackson, cautious but hard-fighting James B Longstreet, impetuous Ambrose P Hill and choleric Daniel H Hill. The skillful co-ordination of these men was to bear much fruit for the South in the summer of 1862.

In June, after the battle of Fair Oaks, the Army of the Potomac was still divided across the Chickahominy; McClellan's men could see the steeples of Richmond, nine miles away. While the bulk of the Federal Army was on the south bank, General Porter remained on the north bank with the V Corps. Porter was ordered to wait there for the arrival of the rest of McDowell's men, who were finally being sent, piecemeal, to reinforce McClellan. Lee saw the vulnerable position of his enemy and realized he was facing a weak general: Richmond had little to fear from McClellan. Jackson was on the way to join forces. It was time to strike.

In those days the eyes of an army were its cavalry, and Lee's foremost horseman was the handsome and flamboyant General J E B ('Jeb') Stuart, whose plumed hat and daring exploits were familiar to soldiers on both sides. Ordered to make a reconnaissance of the Federals, Stuart and 1200 men proceeded to ride completely around the Army of the Potomac, raiding as they went, while Federal cavalry under Stuart's father-in-law, Philip Cook, gave futile pursuit. Spectacular as this raid was, however, it served to alert McClellan to the danger of attack, and he began to arrange his defenses.

After Stuart's report, Lee decided to attack Porter on the north bank – enveloping the Union right –

and drive his forces into the James. The resulting series of clashes came to be known as the Seven Days' Battles.

June 25 saw minor action at Oak Grove, McClellan driving in some Rebel outposts. Next day, at the battle of Mechanicsville, Lee dispatched General Magruder to repeat his theatrics for the benefit of the Federals on the south bank. While Magruder and his small force successfully bemused their opponents into thinking the day of wrath was at hand, Lee,

massing most of his army opposite Porter, initiated a complex plan of attack. But Lee's plans went awry, largely due to the unexpected slowness of Jackson; Porter's men handily repulsed the Confederate offensive. In spite of his victory, however, McClellan decided forthwith to get out of there.

At Gaines's Mill on 27 June, another Southern attempt on Porter's corps did not go as planned, again largely due to Jackson's uncharacteristic indecisiveness. But after a day of hard fighting, the Federals were finally pushed back. McClellan, over-

Confederate General Richard S Ewell, who fought beside 'Stonewall' Jackson in the Shenandoah Valley.

estimating Lee's strength by some 100,000 men, ordered retreat to Harrison's Landing, a Federal supply base on the James River. That night McClellan wrote in fury to his superiors in Washington, 'You have done your best to sacrifice this army.' (This absurd and insubordinate accusation was deleted from the telegram by a decoding clerk before anyone else saw it.)

By 29 June the Army of the Potomac was withdrawing in good order to the southeast. On that and the two following days – at Savage's Station, White Oak Swamp, and Malvern Hill – Lee tried and failed to stop the Federal retreat or turn it into a rout. Lee's whole effort, nonetheless, was a strategic victory for the South: in seven days of hard fighting he had successfully pushed the Federal Army away from Richmond and had squelched the Peninsular Campaign. But on the other hand, he had failed to seriously damage the Army of the Potomac, which settled in good order into Harrison's Landing, protected by Union gunboats. The main reasons for Lee's incomplete success were the superiority of Federal artillery (especially at Malvern Hill) and the inexplicable lethargy of Jackson and his men (who may simply have been exhausted by the Valley Campaign). Federal losses in the Seven Days' Battles were 16,000, Confederate losses 20,000.

As for McClellan – his Peninsular Campaign had

Right: Union General Nathaniel B Banks. *Below*: The Second Battle of Bull Run, or Second Manassas, 29 August 1862.

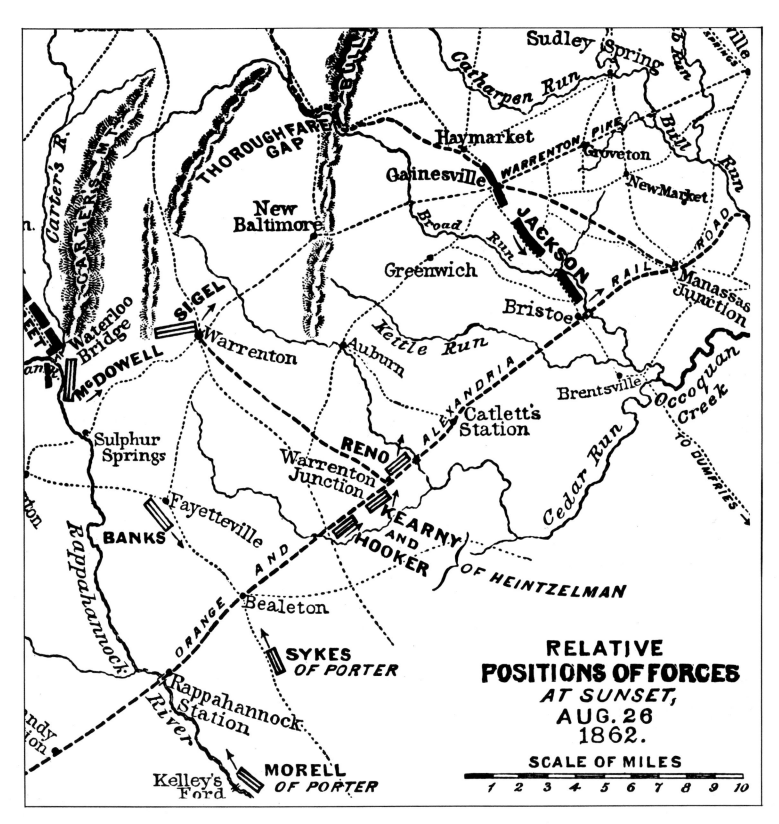

RELATIVE
POSITIONS OF FORCES
AT SUNSET,
AUG. 26
1862.

SCALE OF MILES

1 2 3 4 5 6 7 8 9 10

come within sight of the enemy's capital with vastly superior forces and equipment, and he had there been fooled and outfought. Due to a lack of accurate reconnaissance and aggressive action, he had ultimately accomplished nothing whatever and had lost many men in the process.

Moreover, Union humiliations at the hands of Robert E Lee were not over in this long and tragic summer of 1862. On 29-30 August a Federal Army under General John Pope – 75,696 men from the corps of Banks, Frémont and McDowell – were soundly beaten by 48,527 Southerners in the Second Bull Run, near Manassas, Virginia. Federal casualties were 15,000, the South's 9000. (McClellan was supposed to have combined with Pope's army, but didn't make it.) Pope was relieved at once and his shattered forces merged with the Army of the Potomac.

Thus ended, ingloriously, the Federal invasion of Virginia. In seven months Lee and Jackson had cleared the state of enemy forces for the first time in the war. A Federal Army had been at the gates of Richmond; now it was Lee whose victorious forces were 25 miles from Washington. There seemed only

Positions of the opposing forces on the eve of the Second Battle of Bull Run.

one logical way to extend this extraordinary achievement.

On 3 September Lee notified President Davis that the time was propitious to invade the North through Maryland, and Davis approved the plan. Thereby came Lee's first big mistake: he failed – or refused – to understand that the only hope of the South lay in defense, not in offense.

Lee was dazzled by what could be gained by a successful invasion: it could galvanize anti-war and pro-Southern sentiment in the North, perhaps leading Maryland to secede; it would indirectly threaten Washington; it would keep Union forces out of Lee's beloved Virginia and hamstring Federal operations elsewhere; and perhaps most importantly, it might clinch ongoing efforts to gain English and French recognition of the Confederacy, which if successful could bring vast resources of weapons and supplies to the South.

The Confederate invasion began with the Army of Northern Virginia wading across the Potomac River toward a concentration in Frederick, Maryland, by 7 September. The Army of the Potomac moved slowly northwest in pursuit. Then came another mistake: on 9 September Lee issued Special Order No 191, directing his army to split into two parts. Jackson and six divisions were sent south to capture the Federal garrison at Harper's Ferry, Maryland, at the top of the Shenandoah – this would open the Valley to Southern supply lines and, if necessary, clear a line of retreat. Following this, Jackson was to rejoin Lee. Leaving a screening force under D H Hill to guard the pass at South Mountain, the rest of Lee's army (Longstreet's command) moved north to Hagerstown, Maryland.

This was not the first (or last) time Lee was to violate the old military maxim that forbids dividing forces in the face of the enemy. On other occasions – notably at the Second Bull Run and later at Chancellorsville – this tactic was to produce spectacular

results. But this time Longstreet, always the cautionary critic, advised against Lee's plan: as was to be the case before Gettysburg, Longstreet was right.

Indeed, a mysterious quirk of fate nearly lost Lee his army, and the South the war, before he could take the initiative. On the sunny afternoon of 13 September, while resting in a field, a Federal soldier found in the grass a bulky envelope; inside, incongruously wrapped around two cigars, was a signed copy of Special Order No 191, giving the exact disposition of all Lee's forces. McClellan soon had the order; to General Gibbon he exclaimed, 'Here is a paper with which, if I cannot whip Bobby Lee, I will be willing to go home!' It was the purest gold of all conceivable opportunities.

No one ever figured out who lost the order, but by nightfall Lee had learned from Jeb Stuart that McClellan had it. Knowing that with only a modicum of dispatch McClellan could defeat him in detail, Lee ordered his forces south to join Jackson's.

Opposite: General Thomas J ('Stonewall') Jackson, whose Shenandoah Valley Campaign of 1862 became a model for military strategists. His untimely death in 1863 was a grievous blow to the South.
Above: A Union recruiting poster from the mid-Civil War era.
Left: Senator Charles Sumner of Massachusetts, an outspoken abolitionist and egalitarian whose views earned him enmity in both North and South.

McClellan began to move his army west – faster than usual, but not quite fast enough to capitalize fully on his opportunity. A Union soldier recollected the march:

By daylight next morning we were in motion again – the whole army. The gathering of such a multitude is a swarm, its march a vast migration. It fills up every road leading in the same direction over a breadth of many miles, with long ammunition and supply trains disposed for safety along the inner roads, infantry and artillery next in order outwardly, feelers of cavalry all along its front and far out on its flanks; while behind, trailing along every road for miles . . . are the rabble of stragglers – laggards through sickness or exhaustion, squads of recruits, convalescents from the hospital, special duty men going up to rejoin their regiments.

On 14 September the Army of the Potomac easily broke through Southern defenses at South Mountain. To the south on the same day, Union forces pushed back McLaws' division of Jackson's forces at Crampton's Gap: still Jackson easily took Harper's Ferry on the 15th. However, 'Stonewall' was behind schedule, moving late to rejoin Lee – McClellan still had his chance to interpose between Lee's divided army.

Hearing of Jackson's success, Lee then made an audacious decision – he elected to stand and fight McClellan at Sharpsburg, on Antietam Creek. He had with him 19,000 men, and Jackson would add 40,000 more if he could make it to Sharpsburg in time. The Army of Northern Virginia would then fight with the Potomac River at its back, facing an enemy nearly twice its size and possessing superior artillery. This extraordinary gamble, wagered with his entire army, can perhaps be best explained as indicating Lee's low opinion of McClellan's generalship. If so, Lee was indeed an astute judge of his opponent, as usual, but his calculations did not allow for the fighting spirit of the Army of the Potomac: its men were to prove better soldiers than the leaders with whom they were afflicted.

McClellan moved his army to the east bank of Antietam Creek on 15-16 September. Confederate General Longstreet later wrote of the appearance of the Army of the Potomac:

On the forenoon of the 15th, the blue uniforms of the Federals appeared among the trees that crowned the heights on the eastern bank of the Antietam. The number increased, and larger and larger grew the field of blue until it seemed to stretch as far as the eye could see, and from the tops of the mountains down to the edges of the stream gathered the great army of McClellan. It was an awe-inspiring spectacle as this grand force settled down in sight of the Confederates, then shattered by battles and scattered by long and tiresome marches.

Above: Union General Fitz-John Porter, whose career was destroyed at the Second Battle of Bull Run.
Below: A slain soldier of General Ewell's Corps.

But McClellan remained true to form: on 16 September he squandered another bit of his advantage by spending the day positioning his forces instead of mounting an attack before Jackson arrived late in the afternoon. On the evening of the 16th General Joseph Hooker's men skirmished with John B Hood's Confederates around a little white brick church, of the Dunker sect, in the center of the lines.

It has never been certain exactly what McClellan's plan of attack for 17 September was. As best one can tell, Hooker's I Corps, on the Union right, was to open the attack by moving on Lee's left; Hooker was to be supported by General Joseph K F Mansfield's XII Corps. Meanwhile, General Ambrose E Burnside, commanding the IX Corps on the Union left, was to carry out either a diversion, a secondary attack, or a full-fledged offensive – it was not clear at the time and has not become clear since. In any case, when these assaults on the flanks had developed, General Edwin V Sumner was to lead his II Corps into the Rebel center, penetrating the Southern line. The corps of Generals William B Franklin and Fitz-John Porter were held in reserve to clinch the victory, or cover retreat, as the case might be. It is possible McClellan had a sound plan, but the commanders involved seemed virtually unaware of it. As an inevitable result, the actual attack was confused and piecemeal, developing from right to left of the Union line in three stages.

In following the tumultuous course of the conflict as it developed around the Antietam, it is useful to keep in mind the observations on soldiers in battle that were written later by a participant:

It is astonishing how soon, and by what slight causes, regularity of formation and movement are lost in actual battle. Disintegration begins with the first shot. To the book-soldier, all order seems destroyed, months of drill apparently going for nothing in a few minutes. Next after the most powerful factor in the derangement – the enemy – come natural obstacles and the inequalities of the ground. One of the commonest is a patch of trees. An advancing line lags there inevitably, the rest of the line swinging around insensibly, with the view of keeping the alignment, and so losing direction. The struggle for the possession of such a point is sure to be persistent. Wounded men crawl to a wood for shelter, broken troops reform behind it, a battery planted in its edge will stick there after other parts of the line have given way. Often a slight rise of ground in an open field, not noticeable a thousand yards away, becomes, in the keep of a stubborn regiment, a powerful headland against which the waves of battle roll and break, requiring new dispositions and much time to clear it. A stronger fortress than a casual railroad embankment often proves, it would be difficult to find; and as for a sunken road, what possibilities of victory or disaster lie in that obstruction. At Antietam it was a low, rocky

ledge, prefaced by a cornfield. There were woods, too, and knolls, and there were other cornfields; but the student of that battle knows one cornfield only – *the* cornfield, now historic, lying a quarter of a mile north of Dunker Church.

At first light on 17 September opposing batteries rumbled into action. Surveying the landscape, Federal General Hooker dimly saw the little white Dunker Church on high ground beyond the cornfield, just in front of the West Woods. Hooker realized that the building was the key to everything: take it, and you took the Rebel center and finished Lee. Hooker set his I Corps marching south toward that goal, Doubleday's division descending the Hagerstown Turnpike, Meade's division just to the left, moving into the cornfield, and Rickett's pushing through the East Wood.

These advancing forces quickly ran into trouble, first from Confederate batteries and then from flanking fire out of the West Wood. As the Federals moved into the forty-acre field of head-high corn, they were met by the enemy, and an appalling free-for-all developed: men fought as if maddened and fell by hundreds. As the morning wore on, the fighting swung savagely back and forth between the East and West Woods, always concentrating in the cornfield. General Rickett's 2nd Division, coming out of the East Wood, found in that field the most terrible fire it would ever endure: there fell a third of the division. Meade's division fared similarly in the middle. Both divisions were pushed back, both regrouped and prepared to advance again. General John Gibbon and his Black Hat Brigade – afterward dubbed the Iron Brigade – pushed through heavy fire toward the West Wood and the Dunker Church. (Men walked into the galling fire with heads inclined and averted, grimacing, as if walking into a driving rain.)

Above: The battlefield at Antietam.
Below: Frederick Douglass, a former slave and abolitionist who became the best-known black American of the Civil War era.

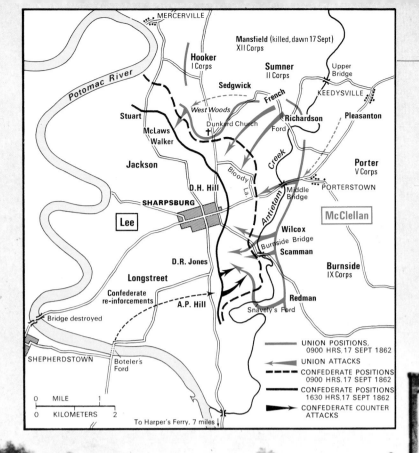

Finally, almost without direction, a jumbled wave of Federal forces swarmed toward the church. After some progress, the Federals ran head-on into a strong counterattack by John B Hood's Texas Brigade – their first hot meal in days had been interrupted and they were enraged and implacable. The Texans' volley struck the Union drive 'like a scythe running through our line'; the Federals turned and ran. Gibbon returned to the Miller farm and organized a Union battery to oppose the charging Rebels, who were met there by double-shotted canister at 50 feet and fell back in their turn. By that time Hooker's corps had suffered nearly 2500 casualties; the Rebels had lost almost half the numbers engaged in that area at the outset. All this for a field of corn and a little church.

Around seven in the morning old General Mansfield began to move his XII Corps in support of Hooker. Mansfield had two divisions, under Generals A S Williams and G S Greene. Like all the Federal commanders on this day, Mansfield had only vague orders and little information: riding with Williams, he pushed slowly through the East Wood to the cornfield. There he rode out to see whether the field held friends or foe; his answer was a bullet in the stomach that wounded him mortally. The fighting then swept back west across the corn, the Confederates withdrew, and another layer of human wreckage was deposited on the bloody field.

Profiting by this Union push, General Greene's brigade made it as far as the West Wood beyond the Dunker Church, and there held on before shattered and exhausted Confederate resistance. Greene had pushed clean through the Confederate line before he had to stop. At that point the battle could have

been clinched, Lee's line broken, his army taken, the war ended. McClellan had 24,000 fresh troops at hand, the corps of Porter and Franklin. But he sent no reinforcements to Greene. Hooker could not help – he had been shot in the foot and carried from the field. His corps was badly cut up and disorganized. The rest of Mansfield's division was tied down by the enemy, so Greene's men pushed no farther.

The I Corps by this time had spent its force, leaving a ghastly harvest on the pastures of small country farms, for possession of which thousands had been maimed and killed. The next act of the battle passed to the II Corps. Around 9:00 PM General Edwin V Sumner, like Mansfield an elderly, white-bearded regular-army commander, led his II Corps into attack, with the divisions of John Sedgwick and William H French (Israel B Richardson's 1st Division lagged behind, for no discernible reason). Like Mansfield before him, Sumner had only a vague idea of what he was supposed to do, and

Opposite: Troop movements in the battle along Antietam Creek. *Below:* A Southern railroad destroyed. The Civil War was the first modern conflict in which railroads played a vital role.

General McClellan's tent at Antietam, the last battle in which he fought. General George Meade took over his command in June of 1863.

still less idea what had happened so far in the battle. As he rode anxiously forward, looking around for Hooker's and Mansfield's forces, Sumner could see no trace of the Union right and deduced to his dismay that the entire right had been destroyed. He was wrong, but this notion was to have its impact on the course of the battle.

Robert E Lee knew very well what was happening so far this day: his left had been stricken and was in imminent danger of collapse. Lee also correctly divined that the next Union push would strike his center. All morning he had been stripping his right, where Union General Burnside was essaying futile assaults, to shore up Confederate lines on the center and left. Scraping the bottom of his supply of reinforcements, Lee ordered McLaws's division, just arrived from Harper's Ferry, to join Walker's division and some of Jubal Early's men in moving to the middle, whence Sumner was now heading.

Sumner's two divisions pushed west at right angles to Hooker's previous offensive, Sedgwick's division sweeping through the cornfield and the West Wood while French's men, behind Sedgwick, wandered off to the left, to be followed eventually by Richardson. Sedgwick's drive was virtually unopposed as they went through the West Wood, immaculately dressed in three lines, sweeping the tatters of Hood's forces before them. Union officers, watching this advance through telescopes at McClellan's headquarters, remarked that nothing could stop them now.

Sedgwick's men emerged from the wood into open fields with no enemy in sight and paused to dress their lines. All was silent. They had marched straight through a gap in the enemy center. Then suddenly, at the last possible moment, Lee's reinforcements arrived and descended like a thunderclap on the Northerners. Shot and shell plowed into the Federals from the left, front and rear. Rebels seemed to spring from the ground and charged savagely; in ten minutes 500 Federals fell without having fired a shot. In the confusion, his men taking fire seemingly from all sides, General Howard of the 2nd Brigade was trying desperately to dress his lines when Sedgwick galloped up and screamed 'My God, Howard, you must get out of here!' But by that time no one needed to be ordered: the division melted away like a spent wave, fled under pursuit back through the woods and through the cornfield. Sedgwick was shot off his horse and 2500 casualties, half the division, remained behind. It had taken just 15 minutes to rout the supposedly unstoppable 2nd Division. Charging across the cornfield in pursuit of Sedgwick, the Rebels met a withering fire from Federal artillery on the eastern slope and came to a halt, finally re-forming to drive Greene back from Dunker Church.

Greene's men retreated east across the fields near the Roulette and Clipp farmhouses, and there found French's advancing division, which pushed the charging enemy back again. It was about 9:30 in the morning. In four hours of fighting nearly 12,000 men had fallen within a thousand-yard-square area. And now French's men were marching into one of the most harrowing engagements of the day.

It began with an almost ludicrous episode: in the Roulette farmyard the 132nd Pennsylvania ran afoul of some bees, whose hives had been hit by a Rebel shell. The Pennsylvanians were nearly routed by a swarm of furious insects. Pressing on, the division found itself on the crest of a slope looking down toward a sunken lane that was bristling with Rebels – D H Hill's men. It was only a rugged, zigzagging country road, worn down by traffic and rain. History would remember it as Bloody Lane.

Green dressed his men into four lines and ordered them down. A Confederate Colonel would recall the approach: 'Their gleaming bayonets flashed like burnished silver in the sunlight. With the precision of step and perfect alignment of a holiday parade this magnificent array moved to the charge.'

The holiday parade met a devastating volley from the road that blasted away the front rank and sent the rest flying back to the crest. There, hugging the ground, they were torn by Southern artillery from high ground across the way. The notion of attacking the little road seemed utterly suicidal.

At length two brigades of Franklin's VI Corps arrived and settled in on the right, covering Greene's flank. Then Israel Richardson's 1st Division moved up, and the hard-fighting Irish Brigade, led by General Thomas F Meagher, was ordered in to meet a Southern flank attack on the left. The opposing charges crashed into one another at point-blank range while Southern artillery opened up enfilade fire from both sides. The Irishmen decided they could do no worse than advance, and slowly pushed the enemy back. Richardson arrived with fresh troops, who pushed past the Irishmen as they came to an exhausted halt.

Painfully, the Federals fought closer and closer;

one Colonel Cross, an old veteran of the Indian wars, ordered his men to paint their faces with soot and led them war-whooping to the charge. The Rebels had finally taken enough and fled from Bloody Lane just after noon. In the lane the Federals found the bodies stacked so deep that it was no longer a sunken road, and neither defensible nor endurable.

Once again the Southern center was teetering on the edge of ruin. Rebel forces were shot to pieces, Hood reporting his division 'dead on the field,' Longstreet in the thick of it commanding devastated troops with no ammunition at all – he turned back several Union charges with two cannons alone. Lee had used every man he could muster. Longstreet

Above: The aftermath of the Battle of Antietam.
Left: Union soldiers signaling by night.

later wrote that 10,000 Federals could have swamped Lee's army then and there.

McClellan still had the men to do it: the comparatively fresh corps of Franklin and Richardson. In fact, he ordered Sumner to attack 'if possible.' Sumner, stunned by the catastrophe his men had suffered and supposing Hooker's entire corps to be ruined, replied to the order, 'Tell General McClellan I have no command!' Over Franklin's protests, Sumner forbade an attack. McClellan, sitting pat at his headquarters – from which he never budged to see things for himself – figured Sumner must know what he was talking about and rescinded the order. Lee's center had held on with a thread, with less than a thread.

By pulling his punch now at the thought of more carnage, McClellan helped to ensure that the carnage would continue for another two and one-half years. The Army of the Potomac had been handed an astonishing series of opportunities over the last few days, and its leaders had wasted them all, one by one. The last chance now lay on the Union left, where Ambrose E Burnside was in command. There was played out the third act of the battle.

As mentioned before, the exact nature of General Burnside's role in McClellan's plan has never been clear to history. Nor was it clear to General Burnside at the time. Was he to mount a strong attack or to sustain a diversion? What was apparently clear in any case to the bewhiskered commander was that he had to get his men across that bridge in front of him, a small stone bridge over the Antietam that chronicles would remember by his name.

Burnside paused before his bridge until ten in the morning, thereby allowing Lee to strip forces from that sector and gain local superiority elsewhere. Perhaps Burnside was mesmerized by the bridge because the enemy had covered it so carefully – Rebel sharpshooters on the west bank of the Antietam had a clear line of fire onto the bridge and all its approaches, and a goodly number of field-pieces were trained on the area as well. Perhaps that is one reason why Burnside never discovered that the Antietam was so shallow it could be waded at almost any point without wetting one's shirt. It simply did not occur to him or anyone else to check it out.

Therefore, he threw his attacking troops into a narrow approach enfiladed in every inch by enemy fire. (He did send General Isaac P Rodman's division downstream to look for a rumored ford: they promptly got lost.) Around ten o'clock in the morning urgent orders came from McClellan to push across the stream. Colonel George Crook was ordered to charge over the bridge with three Ohio regiments; Crook got confused behind some hills and missed the bridge entirely. A while later General Samuel D Sturgis struck out with the 6th New Hampshire and 2nd Maryland; they made it to the approach road but were shot to pieces before reaching the bridge.

By one o'clock in the afternoon McClellan's

The Confederate dead at Antietam.

patience had run out; the bridge was ordered taken at all costs. Colonel Edward Ferrero, of Sturgis's 2nd Division, assembled the 51st New Hampshire and 51st New York and promised them a keg of whiskey if they took the bridge. This apparently did the trick. Covered by all the fire Burnside could muster, these two brigades gallantly pressed over the bridge, losing 500 men, and began to push back the Rebels on the hills beyond. Since Lee had thinned defenses there to only some 2500 infantry and a few cannons, the Union now had one last golden opportunity: envelop the Southern left and take Lee's whole army.

Burnside's bridge was broached at one o'clock: not until three o'clock did he begin a major advance, and that with only one of the four divisions he had at hand – Wilcox's 1st Division. But still he outnumbered the enemy, and his forces slowly pushed the Confederates back to the edge of Sharpsburg, aided by Rodman's brigade which had finally forded the Antietam.

Advancing toward Sharpsburg, driving back last-ditch Southern resistance, General Rodman saw a field of corn on his left. Something about that field looked ominous, and Rodman tried to swing the green troops of the 16th Connecticut to face it. The brigade fell into confusion, just as a murderous volley poured from the cornfield, directed by the forces of General A P Hill, who had that instant arrived after a 17-mile forced march from Harper's Ferry. To complete the Federals' confusion, these Rebels were wearing captured blue uniforms. The Yankees, a moment before dashing to final victory, were being mowed down in hundreds and could not even determine whom to shoot at.

The Federal attack faltered, collapsed. Burnside had two unused divisions and could have turned this last setback and clinched the victory. He didn't even attempt it. A P Hill had saved the Confederacy. Burnside's men retreated back to the ridge west of the creek, and both sides fell exhausted into their positons. The battle was ended.

Behind Union lines a correspondent surveyed a scene of holocaust in Bloody Lane:

The hillside was dotted with prostrate forms of men in blue, but in the sunken road, what a ghastly spectacle! The Confederates had gone down as the grass falls before the scythe. Words are inadequate to portray the scene. Resolution and energy still lingered in the pallid cheeks, in the set teeth, in the gripping hand. I recall a soldier with the cartridge between his thumb and finger, the end of the cartridge bitten off, and the paper between his teeth when the bullet had pierced his heart, and the machinery of life . . . had come to a standstill. A young lieutenant had fallen while trying to rally his men; his hand was still firmly grasping his sword, and determination was visible in every line of his face. I counted fourteen bodies lying together, literally in a heap, amid the corn rows on the hillside. The broad, green leaves were sprinkled and stained with blood.

Casualties were to be the worst of any single day in the entire war: for the North, of 75,316 effectives, there were 2108 dead, 9549 wounded, 753 missing – 12,410 casualties; for the South, of 51,844 effectives, there were 2700 dead, 9024 wounded, 2000 missing – 13,724 casualties.

Seemingly daring McClellan to attack again, Lee stayed in his position until 18 September. Jackson and Longstreet had to convince Lee that a counter-attack was hopeless. Two great armies had stood and battered one another until both were frayed and exhausted. McClellan had capitalized neither on his immense numerical advantage nor on his chain of golden opportunities; during the battle he had also failed to commit 24,000 fresh troops, who could have destroyed Lee's army at almost any point.

Both armies were seriously damaged but would live to fight again. The actual outcome was manifestly a stalemate, one that left nearly 25,000 men dead and maimed. Did anyone 'win'?

Yes: in the long run the North won a significant strategic victory. To begin with, Lee withdrew back to Virginia beginning on 18 September; his invasion had been stymied. The North, remembering the humiliations of both Bull Runs, were content to call it a great victory, and it raised Union spirits measurably.

Perhaps most importantly, the Battle of Antietam gave Abraham Lincoln the chance he had been waiting for to release his Emancipation Proclamation. This epochal document (though it actually freed no slaves at the time) was the beginning of the end of human slavery in the United States. It transformed the public perception of the war from a fight against secession to a crusade against slavery. After that, no European country could recognize the Confederacy without appearing to be on the side of oppression. Henceforth the South had to go it alone, and it lacked the manpower and resources to do that forever.

Lincoln, though, was not fooled by McClellan's 'victory' at Antietam. It was the Young Napoleon's last battle – except the one he later fought and lost at the polls as Lincoln's presidential opponent. But there was still to be a long and agonizing road to travel before the Army of the Potomac found the leadership its fighting spirit deserved.

Above: Clara Barton, foundress of the American National Red Cross, known as 'the angel of the battlefields' to the Union troops she nursed throughout the war.
Below: The Army of the Potomac crosses the Rappahannock.

CHAPTER FOUR
CHANCELLORSVILLE
LEE'S GREATEST VICTORY
AND GREATEST LOSS

THE AUTUMN OF 1862 saw the North's fortunes on the upswing. In September, after the battle of Antietam, Lee pulled back from his invasion of Maryland and Confederate General Braxton Bragg was likewise stymied in Kentucky by William S Rosecrans. The North now had the upper hand for the first time, and needed to play that hand wisely and decisively. In November Lincoln finally accepted the fact that General McClellan was not the man to do so: after six weeks of delay in pursuing Lee after Antietam, the 'Young Napoleon' was relieved as commander of the Army of the Potomac. Hearing this news, Lee mused wryly to Longstreet that he hated to part with McClellan, 'for we always understood each other so well. I fear they may continue to make these changes till they find someone whom I don't understand.' It would be some time, though, before Lee needed to worry on that score: Lincoln's chosen replacement for McClellan was a man destined to become a legend in the history of warfare as one of the most spectacular blunderers of all time: General Ambrose E Burnside.

In his memoirs Grant described Burnside as 'an officer who was generally liked and respected. He was not, however, fitted to command an army. No one knew this better than himself.' A genial and handsome man, Burnside sported an extravagant set of muttonchop whiskers which were perhaps his most enduring legacy – they gave the word 'side-burns' to the language. 'Burn,' as he was affectionately known, *looked* the way most folks thought a general should look. At any rate, Lincoln had offered him command of the Army of the Potomac even before Antietam, but Burnside had modestly declined. In November Lincoln simply brushed aside his protests and assigned him the command. (Lincoln settled on Burnside partly because there were various military and civilian objections to General Joseph Hooker, the logical choice for the job, and partly because Burnside's inept performance at Antietam was somehow seen as a success).

So Burnside went dutifully to work, producing a plan to take Richmond by crushing Lee at Fredericksburg, Virginia, on the banks of the Rappahannock River. The plan was certainly workable when the Army of the Potomac arrived at the town on 17 November: at that time Lee's Army of Northern Virginia was divided and greatly outnumbered. But then Burnside dallied for nearly a month while Lee concentrated and dug his forces into position just behind the town. From these impregnable defenses Lee looked forward to the coming Federal attack with manifest delight. This anticipation was well founded. On 13 December Burnside unleashed a series of suicidal frontal attacks on the Confederate lines, attacks that left piles of Union dead in front of Marye's Heights and finally accounted for 12,700 casualties to the South's 5300.

Previous spread: The Battle of Chancellorsville, May 1863.
Below: A Union division charges at the Battle of Fredericksburg.

After this tragic debacle Burnside made one more effort to do his job, this time by marching the army upstream to cross the Rappahannock in hopes of striking Lee's flank. But this operation began squarely in the middle of the usual January thaw, with its accompanying torrents of rain; during it the entire Army of the Potomac nearly disappeared into an apparently bottomless sea of mud. This Mud March, as history would call it, was soon aborted and the bedraggled and demoralized troops slogged back to their camps across the river from Lee at Fredericksburg. Burnside had thus crowned a debacle with a fiasco. He was relieved at his own request on 25 January 1863.

Now General Joseph Hooker, called 'Fighting Joe' by the press, got the nod as new commander of the Army of the Potomac. His friends in Washington had overcome political opposition to the appointment and Hooker genuinely wanted the job – indeed, he had schemed to get it. Both his supporters and detractors agreed that there were two Joe Hookers – one an experienced, dashing and hard-fighting general; the other fond of verbally sniping at his superiors and conniving for his own benefit, and equally fond of the bottle and the ladies.

Once in command, however, Hooker suddenly revealed unsuspected, McClellan-like abilities as an organizer. He repaired the Army of the Potomac from the ground up, improving the food supply, hospital care, and sanitation of his troops, and drilling them incessantly. The intelligence service was reorganized with the result of fewer exaggerated estimates of enemy strength like those that had plagued McClellan. The pride and morale of the army rose with its physical condition and its numbers: by spring 1863 there were 122,000 infantry, 12,000 men in a well-trained cavalry and 400 cannons. It was the most powerful army the country had ever seen, and it was ready for anything. Hooker crowed confidently to his superiors, 'May God have mercy on General Lee, for I will have none!'

In April Lee's Army of Northern Virginia still lay in Fredericksburg, across the Rappahannock from the Army of the Potomac. To take Lee's army, Hooker devised a plan that was both imaginative and sound – leaving a force to hold Lee in position, Hooker would march the bulk of his troops around Fredericksburg in a wide strategic envelopment, coming in behind Lee from the west. The Confederates could then either sit and be destroyed or retreat and thus expose their flank to the Federals.

With the addition of cavalry capable (it was supposed) of dealing with Jeb Stuart, Hooker prepared his campaign by sending General George Stoneman's 12,000 horsemen on a raid to Lee's rear, where they were ordered to cut Southern supply lines. The division left on 13 April and soon ran into floods that held them up until the 27th, after which they ranged around to little purpose. As one trooper remembered, 'Our only accomplishments were the burning of a few canal boats . . . some bridges, hen roosts, and tobacco houses.' With his usual acumen,

Lee simply ignored Stoneman.

On 27 April Hooker struck camp, leaving 40,000 men under Sedgwick (the VI Corps, plus Reynolds's I Corps) in Lee's front, and moving the rest northwest and then south across fords on the Rappahannock and Rapidan. By 30 April these forces – 80,000 men, the corps of Generals Darius N Couch (II), Henry W Slocum (XII), Daniel E Sickles (III), George G Meade (V), and Oliver O Howard (XI) – were gathered around Chancellorsville, an insignificant road crossing sporting a mansion where Hooker established his headquarters. Next day the Federals began marching toward Fredericksburg, ready to take the Rebels by surprise.

However, Robert E Lee had no intention of playing his assigned part in Hooker's little game. For weeks Lee had expected some such move from 'those people,' as he called the Union Army, and on 30 April Jeb Stuart notified him that Federals were moving from Chancellorsville on the Southern rear. At that time Lee had available some 60,000 men, less than half his enemy's strength (Longstreet and Hood were gone foraging in Virginia with a large detachment). Nonetheless, Lee boldly split his army again to meet the Federal threat. A screening force of 10,000 men under General Jubal Early was left to hold Sedgwick at Fredericksburg and ordered to build many fires to fool the Yankees. Lee and Stonewall Jackson marched northwest on 1 May to deal with Hooker.

The road crossing at Chancellorsville was in a small clearing within a large area of dense woods and

Above: Union General George G Meade, appointed commander of the Army of the Potomac in June 1863.

Following pages: Log fortifications of a type widely used in the war.

Above: A double line of Union breastworks in the Wilderness.
Below: Union General E E Ellsworth, an early hero of the war.
Right: Union General Joseph ('Fighting Joe') Hooker, who was badly wounded at Antietam but went on to fight at Fredericksburg and Chancellorsville.

tangled undergrowth known as the Wilderness. Hooker had seen the necessity of pushing past these woods to meet Lee on open ground, where superior Federal artillery would have room to function and the army room to maneuver. On May Day morning Hooker's forces pulled away from Chancellorsville into open country, exactly where Hooker wanted to meet the enemy. The corps of Slocum and Meade led the way, with Couch, Sickles and Howard waiting to follow. Everything was going according to plan: Fredericksburg lay less than a dozen miles away.

Then, on high ground some two miles from Chancellorsville, around 10:30 in the morning, Federal skirmishers ran into a line of Rebel skirmishers from Anderson and McLaws' forces. As one Union soldier remembered, 'There they stood facing each other, steady and silent, gazing, the one in apparent wonderment, the other in real surprise at the unexpected situation.' General George Sykes moved up his division of Meade's corps and began firing, forcing the Rebels back. Hearing the fire, Hooker sent Couch forward in support. All that seemed needed was to form the Union corps in line of battle and sweep the Rebels back toward Fredericksburg.

However, at this first brush with the enemy that was not part of his plan, Joe Hooker began to act like a beaten man. After several hours of inactivity, he ordered all his forces to pull back into the Wilderness toward Chancellorsville and there to dig in. Couch and Meade were furious and protested to Hooker, but he resolutely refused to listen. As for the men, one recalled, 'The soldiers were as discomfited as if they had been checked by a serious repulse. All enthusiasm vanished, all the bright hopes of success disappeared. Before the discharge of a single gun . . . somebody had again blundered.'

Hooker pulled his army back and began to entrench among the tangled woods; meanwhile, he ordered Reynolds's I Corps to come over from the

front of Fredericksburg. As the Federals fell back to Chancellorsville, the Confederates moved up, firing occasionally and probing the Union defenses until the evening. Hooker had made a fatal pause; now the initiative was on the Confederate side. During the afternoon of 1 May, Jeb Stuart's cavalry had moved freely around the Union Army, and late in the day Stuart reported to Lee that the Federal right was vulnerable, 'in the air' with no real protection on the flank.

The Confederates slept that night on the field. Waking in the early morning, one of Lee's staff saw in the dim light 'bending over a scant fire of twigs, two men seated on old cracker boxes and warming their hands over the little fire.' They were Jackson and Lee, planning yet another unpleasant surprise for Joe Hooker. It was to fall upon that luckless right flank, the XI Corps of Oliver O Howard.

On the morning of 2 May the Union Army was well fortified and easily handled the probing attacks of the Rebels on their front. Hooker's lines were roughly in a U-shape, Meade on the left, Slocum and Couch in the middle with Sickles just behind, and Howard on the right. Hooker rode out from his headquarters in the Chancellor mansion to check Howard's entrenchments; viewing them, he commented, 'How strong, how strong!'

Around noon Sickles noticed a large enemy force moving to the right beyond the thick woods on the Union front. Hooker, wondering at first if they were indeed headed for his right flank, sent a cautionary note to Howard. But then Hooker began to convince himself that Lee must be retreating. When Sickles asked permission to move against the enemy, Hooker agreed. Sickles moved out with difficulty through the thick forest and made contact with the end of the Confederate column, capturing some 500 men of the 27th Georgia Infantry. As these prisoners were being led to the rear, some were heard to jeer at the Yanks, 'You'll catch hell before night. You wait until Jackson gets around on your right!' The Federals ignored these threats. Meanwhile Hooker stripped his right flank of Barlow's division and sent them to help Sickles pursue the supposedly retreating Rebels. As Sickles pulled away he left the rest of the XI Corps isolated and unsupported.

During the afternoon the XI Corps became nervous: many of them were Germans who spoke little or no English. Largely for that reason, they were the Cinderella outfit of the army, with an undeserved reputation for running away from battle. The rest of the men scornfully called them 'the Dutchmen,' and they had been put on the right to keep them out of trouble. As the afternoon wore on the men sensed something big was massing beyond the woods. Appeals began going from the front to Howard and to Hooker's staff, asking for help; the appeals were received with derision – the enemy was certainly retreating, there was no threat whatever to the right.

At six o'clock in the afternoon, the advance posi-

tions of the XI Corps were startled to see a mass of rabbits and deer scampering out of the woods toward them. The men whooped and laughed as the animals bolted toward the rear. Scattered shots followed and cannon suddenly appeared on the front; from thousands of throats rose the hair-raising screech of the Rebel yell. Then 26,000 of Stonewall Jackson's men came crashing into the Federal flank in a front a mile wide and four divisions deep, all of them shooting and screaming like demons. Jackson had marched 16 miles through the Wilderness in broad daylight, right in front of the Union Army.

The Rebels moved straight down the trenches, the 9000 men of the XI Corps fleeing in panic before them. Amid the rout was General Howard 'in the middle of the roads and mounted, his maimed arm embracing a stand of colors . . . while with his sound arm he was gesticulating to the men to make a stand by their flag. With bared head he was pleading with his soldiers, literally weeping as he entreated the unheeding horde.' Hooker knew nothing of the rout until he heard an aide screaming 'My God, here they come!' and the rabble of terrified men and horses flooded into the Chancellorsville clearing.

Leaping onto his horse, Hooker rode forward, taking with him Berry's division of the I Corps, whom he ordered to 'Receive 'em on your bayonets!' Berry's men and the XII Corps artillery shoved through the fleeing men and hit the charging Rebels obliquely, slowing their advance on the left and center. Seeing a stand of Union artillery was in danger of being overrun on the right, General Alfred Pleasonton ordered Major Peter Keenan to charge his 8th Pennsylvania Cavalry into the Rebels, to buy time to turn the guns around. Keenan accepted the order knowing it was virtually suicidal. So the cavalrymen, many of them scraped up from a poker game with no idea what was happening, rode directly into the middle of the enemy charge, brandishing their sabers, and rattled the Confederates long enough for Pleasonton to turn the cannon around. Keenan went down with 13 bullets in his body and scores of saddles were emptied. (It was this charge that would make the Confederates leery of men on horseback that night, a fact that would soon make for a disaster to the South.)

Pleasonton got 22 pieces into position and poured canister into the charging Rebels. At Fairview Cemetery Hooker had 36 more guns pelting the enemy. The Rebel advance slowed and halted, the troops becoming disorganized in the growing dark. Over in Hazel Grove, the 15,000 men of Sickles's III Corps had been cut off by Jackson's charge, and as night fell they began fighting their way back to their lines; after a hot and confused struggle in the gloom, with men falling from their own side's fire, part of the corps made it back while the rest settled into an uneasy bivouac in Hazel Grove.

At nine o'clock, amid the confusions of nighttime action, came the accident that was to temper Lee's greatest victory with an irreplaceable loss. Stonewall Jackson had ridden out scouting from his lines

just west of Chancellorsville, to try and find a way to cut off any Federal retreat during the night. He and his party rode into a group of resting Union infantry and wheeled under fire to gallop back down the road. Hearing guns and horsemen approaching, Confederates on both sides of the road opened fire; two of Jackson's party fell dead from their horses and Jackson reeled in the saddle with three wounds. Taken from his horse and placed on a litter, Jackson with his bearers came under heavy artillery fire before they could reach an ambulance. That night Jackson's left arm was amputated and he began slowly to sink.

Also during the night, Federals bivouacking near Chancellorsville began to hear a strange, muffled firing. It was soon discovered, to the men's horror, that the Wilderness was burning and the woods were full of wounded men: the sound was that of exploding muskets and cartridge cases. Soldiers dashed into the woods and removed the few wounded they could reach. Then the survivors stood and listened: 'Curses and yells of pain, piteous appeals and spasmodic prayers could be distinguished. . . . The flames roared more fiercely, the cries grew fainter, until at last they were hushed.'

In spite of the disaster of 2 May, the next dawn brought new opportunities for the Union Army. After their extraordinary attack, Jackson's men were nonetheless in a dangerous position – their commander lay wounded and masses of Federals threatened both their flanks. But Hooker, manifestly outgeneraled on 2 May, remained confused and despondent. On the Confederate side Jeb Stuart took over Jackson's forces, rallied the men with the name of their stricken leader and mounted a savage attack at five in the morning. Stuart caught the III Corps in motion back toward their lines and pushed them out of high ground at Hazel Grove, whence 30 Rebel cannon were brought to bear on Chancellorsville. The clearing quickly became a maelstrom of shot and shell. Then the Rebels began shoving the enemy back toward the Rappahannock.

Late on the previous evening Hooker had sent a dispatch to Sedgwick ordering him to push past the enemy at Fredericksburg and move on Lee's rear at Chancellorsville. The next morning Sedgwick mounted a series of assaults on Early's men at Marye's Heights, where Burnside had been so tragically repulsed in December, and finally stormed the position with heavy losses by 11 in the morning. Sedgwick then moved toward Chancellorsville, hoping to catch Lee in a vise.

On the front porch of his Chancellor mansion headquarters, General Hooker stood amid the furious enemy fire that was smashing his batteries one by one. As he leaned on a pillar, straining for the sound of Sedgwick's approach, Hooker was thrown to the ground by a shell that splintered the pillar. Dazed, he gave Couch temporary command and ordered a withdrawal to entrenchments already prepared in an arc between the Rapidan and the Rappahannock. The Rebels pursued this with-

Opposite: Artillery going into action on the Rappahannock River, 4 June 1863.

Above: The 34-star flag of 1861, under which Union troops fought the first half of the war. President Lincoln refused to have the stars of the Southern states removed from the flag.

Above: Marye's
Heights,
Fredericksburg,
Virginia, taken by
Sedgwick's 6th Maine
Infantry on 3 April
1863.
Right: The levee at
Vicksburg, Mississippi,
a vital Confederate
position commanding
'the Father of Waters.'

drawal, their cannon firing everything they could lay hands on – including old railroad iron, chains and tools. The woods burned again, consuming the dead and wounded of both sides.

A frantic horseman, chaplain of a Mississippi brigade, appeared before Lee announcing Sedgwick's advance from Fredericksburg. Lee calmly told the rider to rest and then put the finishing touch on his masterpiece. Leaving Stuart with 25,000 men to hold Hooker's dug-in 75,000, Lee marched 20,000 to confront Sedgwick's advance on his rear.

Sedgwick ran into General Lafayette McLaws's troops around Salem Church on that afternoon of 3 May. By next morning Lee had surrounded Sedgwick on three sides with McLaws, R H Anderson, and Early, while also reoccupying Marye's Heights with William Barksdale's men. Sedgwick was driven back to Banks's Ford on the Rappahannock, where the Rebels harassed him strongly. The Federals withdrew across the ford on the night of 4 May.

Lee began planning an all-out offensive against Hooker's remaining divisions for 6 May, an offensive that might well have been a disaster for the South given the strength of the Federal entrenchments. But Hooker had already had enough. Over the objections of most of his staff, he withdrew across the Rappahannock during the miserably wet and muddy night of 5 May.

Joe Hooker had gone into battle with a better than two-to-one advantage and had nonetheless let his forces be outnumbered in every encounter: 30,000 Union troops had never been committed at all. Years later Hooker was to make a simple confession about himself at Chancellorsville: 'To tell the truth, I just lost confidence in Joe Hooker.'

Once again the Army of the Potomac had marched to battle with overwhelming strength and glorious hopes; once again their leaders had not been up to the task. The army had been outmaneuvered and soundly thrashed. Union prospects were grim in the Eastern Theater (both Grant and Rosecrans had bogged down in the West as well). Union morale had sunk to a new low while the Army of Northern Virginia had grown exultant. Yet as the Army of the Potomac slogged away from another defeat, they were not entirely demoralized. By now they were soldiers in deed as well as in imagination. They had no illusions left about the nature of war; they knew the dead were just as dead in victory or defeat. Perhaps they also knew now that, with proper leadership, they could fight as well as their enemy.

And impressive as Lee's victory seemed, it was a Pyrrhic victory. Casualty figures are uncertain: Lee had lost about 12,821 killed, missing and wounded to the Union's 17,278. But while the Federals had lost 13 percent of their army, Lee had lost 22 percent of his. Numbers were beginning to count in the war: the South's supply of manpower was limited and becoming more critical with every battle won or lost. The time would come when Southern losses simply could not be replaced.

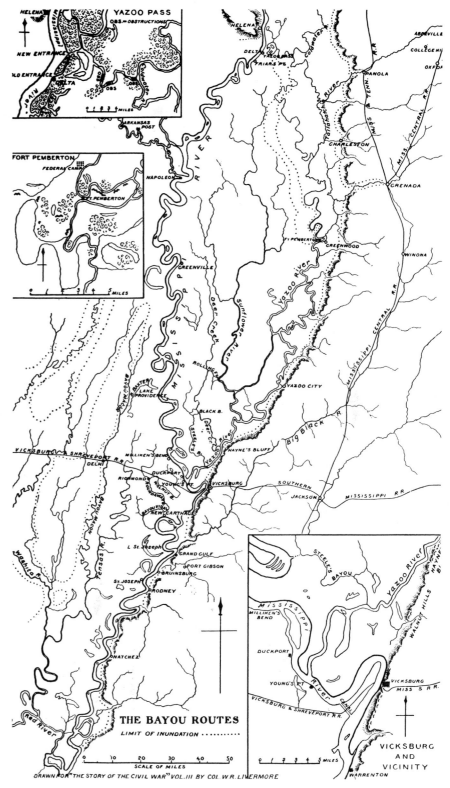

THE BAYOU ROUTES
LIMIT OF INUNDATION ··········
SCALE OF MILES
DRAWN FOR "THE STORY OF THE CIVIL WAR" VOL.III BY COL. W R. LIVERMORE

VICKSBURG AND VICINITY

On 10 May Stonewall Jackson cried out in delirium from his bed, 'Order A P Hill to prepare for action – pass the infantry to the front rapidly – tell Major Hawks . . . .' Then, after a silence, 'No, let us cross over the river and rest under the shade of the trees.' On that enigmatic word of peace the great fighter died, and with him died another large part of the South's hopes.

Nonetheless, Lee was now to turn his sights to the North again, this time past Maryland to Pennsylvania, where the mounting trajectory of his army's fortunes would reach its zenith at the little town of Gettysburg.

Vicksburg and vicinity, showing details of the Bayou Routes (heavily flooded in the winter of 1862-63), Fort Pemberton and the Yazoo Pass.

CHAPTER FIVE
VICKSBURG
THE OPENING OF THE MISSISSIPPI

AS ROBERT E LEE WAS dominating the Eastern Theater of the war with his tactical genius on the battlefield, a different kind of military genius was demonstrating his brilliance in long-range strategic planning in the Western Theater. The man was Ulysses S Grant; the complex and historic Vicksburg Campaign of 1862-63 would be remembered as Grant's masterpiece, as Chancellorsville was Lee's.

The town of Vicksburg, Mississippi, lies atop high bluffs on the banks of the Mississippi River. It occupies the first high land on the eastern bank of the river below Memphis, some 400 miles to the north. Throughout the winter of 1862-63 the Mississippi was swollen by heavy rains, and Vicksburg overlooked hundreds of miles of flooded and swampy land and river bottom. The town was approachable by land only from the east, from Confederate territory. And the water route was impassable to most Union shipping: the bluffs before Vicksburg were bristling with fortifications and batteries that dominated the river below.

Strategically, Vicksburg was one of the two most vital towns of the Confederacy, the other being the rail center of Chattanooga. To the east through Vicksburg came food, supplies and cotton necessary to the Southern war effort. Could the North conquer the city, those supplies would be cut off and Union armies and supplies could pass unmolested through the very center of the Confederacy. It was essential to the North's grand strategy to accomplish that task.

On 25 October 1862 Ulysses S Grant was given command of the Federal Department of the Tennessee. A week after his appointment he began to move overland on Vicksburg. Much of the Mississippi already lay in Union hands – Admiral Farragut had conquered New Orleans in the spring of 1862 and cleared the river up to Baton Rouge, Louisiana. Soon after, a Federal flotilla had all but destroyed a Confederate fleet on the Mississippi at Memphis and taken that city.

In November Grant moved his 40,000 men out of Jackson, Tennessee, marching south on the east side of the Mississippi toward Vicksburg. This campaign soon came to grief: on 20 December a Confederate cavalry force under General Earl van Dorn swept into the Federal base at Holly Springs, Mississippi, just south of the Tennessee border, and destroyed most of Grant's supplies. At the same time, cavalry under Nathan Bedford Forrest raided Union communication lines in western Tennessee, destroying 60 miles of railroad. The Union advance ground to a halt just as further misfortunes developed to the south.

William T Sherman, Grant's closest subordinate, had been dispatched down the Yazoo River to take possession of the landings at Vicksburg, in support of Grant's campaign. But just north of the city at

Previous spread: The siege of Vicksburg, the major achievement of Ulysses S Grant's career. The Union victory at Vicksburg made the defeat of the Confederacy inevitable.
Below: Confederate fortifications at Vicksburg were seven months in the making. They formed a line nine miles long, with nine forts as strong points.

Chickasaw Bluffs, Sherman's forces were severely repulsed on 27-29 December; in that action the Union suffered 1776 casualties to the South's 207. It became clear to Federal leaders that Vicksburg was going to be a tough nut indeed to crack.

Thus at the beginning of 1863 the North's war effort was stalled all over the map: Grant was apparently going nowhere, and neither were Hooker in the East or Rosecrans in Tennessee. Grant proceeded to size up his situation. An overland advance on Vicksburg had just been proven impossible, and the high waters made all land operations difficult, but public and political pressure from the North obliged him to do *something* – or else. Accordingly, Grant shifted his base to Young's Point, nearly opposite Vicksburg on the western (Louisiana) bank of the river, and in the first months of 1863 indulged in a series of experiments that he doubted would work. But they might, who knows, accomplish something – and would satisfy all concerned that he was doing his job.

The first experiment was to cut a canal across Young's Point, in hopes of moving Union boats through it and down the Mississippi, thus bypassing a hairpin turn in the river at Vicksburg – Union boats trying to negotiate that turn would come under fearful fire from Rebel batteries. But the canal when finished could not be filled to a depth sufficient to float the ships.

While the canal was in progress Grant dispatched General James B McPherson's XVII Corps to try and open a passage from Lake Providence south through the soggy landscape, to come out on the Red River south of Vicksburg, whence steamers could move back upstream. This scheme was abandoned in March for a more promising one in the Yazoo Pass, 325 miles north of Vicksburg. There the Federals cut through a levee and the fleet steamed into the Tallahatchie River, moving south toward the Yazoo and Vicksburg. This expedition ran afoul of a hastily constructed Rebel work named Fort Pemberton in honor of Vicksburg's commander, General John C Pemberton. For six days in mid-March the little fort turned back the best efforts of the Federal fleet to pass. Grant then moved on to his fourth and final experiment, an attempt to push Federal ships north through a tangled mass of streams and backwaters called Steele's Bayou. Trying to move up through the tiny waterways to the Yazoo, Admiral David D Porter's boats were obstructed by trees, some of them felled by the Confederates, who then attacked the Union boats on 19 March. Porter had to be rescued by Sherman's corps. There ended Grant's experiments, all of them fantastically difficult and roundabout ways to traverse the few miles that separated Vicksburg from the Union base, which was now at Millikin's Bend just across the river from Vicksburg.

Grant had tried every possible water route to Vicksburg: now he had to go overland, and do it soon – the whole progress of the war in the West was on his shoulders, and the West was where the Con-

federacy must ultimately be beaten – in its own territory. So Grant devised a new plan. The high water had receded enough so that he could march his men south on the Louisiana side of the river. Once south of Vicksburg, they had somehow to cross the Mississippi, which could be done only by running the Federal fleet directly past the fearsome Vicksburg batteries; the ships would meet the army downriver and ferry the troops across. (Admiral Farragut had moved ships past the batteries in the summer of 1862, so perhaps it was possible.) If this could be done, Grant would then move his men northwest across Mississippi, cut communications between Vicksburg and the Confederacy and lay siege to the city. Meanwhile, to screen the operation, Sherman and Colonel R H Grierson would pursue diversionary operations, Sherman on Haines's Bluff near Vicksburg and Grierson moving his cavalry south from Tennessee through Mississippi. Thus Grant planned four carefully coordinated operations – his army, Porter's fleet, Sherman's corps and Grierson's cavalry – involving many thousands of men and horses, a fleet of ships and thousands of square miles of land. To take Vicksburg, many things had to work perfectly in concert, and Washington had to co-operate as well.

This latter element of Grant's requirements was as undependable as any. He had already run afoul of a secret river expedition on Vicksburg planned in Washington by a politically appointed Volunteer general, John A McClernand: this expedition was in effect competing with Grant's for the same prize.

Top: Union Admiral David D Porter, who ran the gauntlet of Confederate batteries at Vicksburg with 12 gunboats and transports to link up with Grant's army at Hard Times, Mississippi (16 April 1863).
Above: Admiral Andrew Foote of the Union Navy, who headed naval operations on the upper Mississippi until March 1862, when he was badly wounded in an assault on the Confederate fort on Island Number 10.

aboard remembered vividly that harrowing passage:

The whole night seemed one terrific roar of cannon. Burning houses made the river almost as light as day. We saw the people in the streets of the town running and gesticulating as if all were mad. Their men at the batteries loaded and fired and yelled as if every shot sank a steamboat. On the west side of the river the lagoons and canebrakes looked weird and dangerous. The sky above was black, lighted only by sparks from the burning houses. Down on the river it was a sheet of flame. One of the steamers and a few of the barges had caught fire and were burning up, the men escaping in lifeboats and by swimming to the western shore.

The musketry on the shore barked and bit at

Above: The USS *Mississippi*, which ran aground and burned in the Union effort to bypass Southern defenses at Port Hudson, Louisiana, en route to Vicksburg.
Right: A Union mortar fires on Confederate shore batteries in the struggle for the Mississippi.
Below: Union General Crocker charges a hilltop position during the siege of Vicksburg.

Having kept Grant in the dark for some time about McClernand, General-in-Chief Halleck finally scotched that expedition and put McClernand's forces under Grant – to McClernand's considerable chagrin. On 29 March Grant sent McClernand's XIII Corps to forge a trail from Millikin's Bend south to New Carthage. The men set about tearing down plantation homes, and anything else handy, to build bridges across the tangled waterways on the Louisiana side. Admiral Porter stood by to provide troop transport and supplies.

By 16 April it was time for the first critical gamble of the campaign – running Union ships past Vicksburg. The ships, six gunboats and several transports of Admiral Porter's fleet, were manned by a few volunteers; in the holds waited men with boards, cotton and gunny sacks to patch up holes made by enemy fire. The vulnerable transport ships were padded with cotton bales and had barges of coal and forage lashed alongside. Around 11:00 PM the ships began floating silently downstream. An hour later they were opposite Vicksburg, where they were spotted by the Confederate defenders. The Rebel batteries opened up, turning the bluffs into a sheet of flame, and the ships put on steam. One of the men

the unprotected pilots on the boats. Ten-inch cannon and great columbiads hurled their shot and shell into the cotton breastworks of the barges or through the rigging of the steamers. The gunboats trembled from the impact of shot against their sides, and at times the little steamers were caught in the powerful eddies of the river and whirled three times around, right in front of the hot-firing batteries.

Porter ran the batteries, losing only one ship and a few barges: the battered flotilla came to rest at Hard

Times, where Grant's army was gathering. On 22 April more transports and barges ran the gauntlet. Meanwhile, Sherman made a feint at Haines's Bluff, moving his corps up and down the river and the shore until Pemberton, in Vicksburg, was convinced a major attack was coming there. Once the Confederates were properly distracted, Sherman marched to join Grant below Vicksburg.

Much as Pemberton was confused by the feint at Haines's Bluff, however, he was more concerned by the other Federal diversion designed to screen Grant's crossing of the Mississippi. General Benjamin H Grierson and 1700 cavalrymen left LaGrange, Tennessee, on 17 April, riding south through Mississippi. A worried Pemberton sent cavalry in pursuit (at the same time marching men to meet Sherman's imaginary offensive at Haines's Bluff). After two weeks of hard riding, evading pursuers, raiding and skirmishing, Grierson arrived at Federally held Baton Rouge on 2 May. His men had ridden 600 miles in 16 days, accounted for 100 Rebel casualties, taken 500 prisoners, destroyed 50 miles of railroad and much enemy weaponry, captured 1000 horses and mules – and suffered only 24 casualties. It was to be remembered as one of the most brilliant cavalry exploits of the war. (This was especially notable since the Union had been having cavalry troubles from the beginning – far fewer Northerners than Southerners were accustomed to the saddle when the war started.)

Grant, meanwhile, had run into resistance trying to cross his troops at Grand Gulf, where on 29 April 17 gunboats failed to reduce a Confederate garrison. Moving a little farther south, Grant crossed his army unopposed at Bruinsburg the next day. The Confederates then pulled out of Grand Gulf and met Grant's overland advance at Port Gibson on 1 May. In a day of fighting amid hills and deep ravines, Grant flanked the 8000 Confederates and brushed them out of the way before their reinforcements could arrive. The Northern forces – the corps of Sherman (XV), McPherson (XVII) and McClernand (XIII) – then pushed northeast across Mississippi, skirmishing constantly with Rebel forces in the rear.

Grant was planning so far to march south and join General Nathaniel P Banks (another politically appointed general of volunteers, who at the outbreak of the war was Governor of Massachusetts) in moving on Confederate-held Port Hudson, on the Mississippi to the south. Learning that Banks was busy with what was to become the extensive – and ill-fated – Red River Campaign, Grant made a bold change in plans that was destined to elevate him to the ranks of the great generals in history. Against the advice of his staff, he decided to cut away from his supply and communications lines and move into the rear of Vicksburg, first taking Jackson, the capital of the state, in the east. Then, having taken care of any potential enemy reinforcements to Vicksburg, he would besiege the city. In military terms, he would *defeat the enemy in detail* before they

had the chance to concentrate superior forces against him. His army would march with all the supplies it could carry and would forage in the countryside; now Southern civilians would have to bear directly the cost of war.

Grant's opponent in Jackson was one of the best generals in the Confederacy – Joseph E Johnston. He had somewhat recovered from his wounds at Fair Oaks and was desperately trying to accumulate enough forces to oppose Grant. Arriving in Jackson the evening of the 13th, Johnston was so ill that he did much of his work in bed.

As Grant moved toward Jackson he sent a detachment to feint toward Vicksburg, where Pemberton was still trying to figure out what the Federals were up to. Sherman crossed his corps at Grand Gulf on 6 May, and by the 12th Grant was approaching

Jackson with 44,000 men. That day McPherson's corps routed a Rebel detachment at Raymond, Mississippi; leaving McClernand in that town to protect his rear, Grant arrived before Jackson on the 13th. That night Johnston wrote to Pemberton in Vicksburg, ordering him to move on Grant's rear.

Johnston had only 6000 men to oppose the Federals' two corps; Confederate reinforcements were on the way, but Grant had no intention of waiting for their arrival, or for Pemberton to move. On 14 May McPherson and Sherman easily stormed Jackson: that night Grant slept in the room Johnston had occupied the night before. Johnston moved his troops north, writing the recalcitrant Pemberton to cut Grant's supply line and then join forces.

But Pemberton had two problems with this order: one, Grant in fact had no supply line, and Pemberton wasted a day trying to find it; two, Confederate President Davis had ordered Pemberton to stay in Vicksburg. Thus Pemberton, already perplexed, was caught between contradictory orders from his government and from his superior, Johnston. He managed to satisfy neither very well.

Having first spent a fruitless 15 May looking for the nonexistent Union supply line to the south, Pemberton then turned his troops around and went

Admiral Porter's ships running the batteries at Vicksburg by night. The fleet was heavily damaged, but only the transport *Henry Clay* was sunk.

Above: Confederate General John C Pemberton, the commander at Vicksburg.
Below: A Thomas Nast drawing for *Harper's Weekly.* Union soldiers halting for a rest.

east to join Johnston. The Confederate troops were exhausted, having marched in every direction for days without finding the enemy. Grant had already foreseen the Confederate move and gone with McClernand and McPherson to meet Pemberton. (Sherman was left in Jackson to destroy manufacturing centers and railroads, a task which, as always, he performed with a vengeance.) At Champion's Hill, a small knoll in the countryside between Vicksburg and Jackson, the forces of Grant and Pemberton collided on 16 May.

Champion's Hill saw the hardest day's fighting of the campaign. The forces engaged were not radically unequal: Grant had 29,000 men of McPherson's and McClernand's corps, and Pemberton some 22,000 (Sherman, ordered out of Jackson in the morning, arrived after the battle). McClernand made contact with the Rebel left flank about 9:30 AM; however, he waited over four hours to make what should have been the initial attack. This gave Pemberton time to shift troops to meet McPherson's assault on his right flank at about eleven. Had McClernand attacked promptly in the morning the Federals could probably have overwhelmed Pemberton's army and marched unopposed into Vicksburg. The fighting surged back and forth indecisively for hours, Champion's Hill changing hands repeatedly. At one point Logan's division of McPherson's corps moved

on the rear of the Confederate right, cutting off Pemberton's only road of retreat; Grant, not knowing this, uncovered the road again by moving these troops to reinforce his center. Pemberton soon made use of the road, pulling his forces back just after three in the afternoon. The Confederates withdrew, bedraggled but in fair order, to the Big Black River, closely pursued by Grant's men. The casualties in the day's fighting at Champion's Hill were 2441 for the Union, 3851 for the South. Grant points out in his memoirs that Pemberton should then have evacuated Vicksburg and marched north to join Johnston; this in fact was what Johnston, knowing Vicksburg was now doomed in any case, wanted Pemberton to do. Instead, Pemberton pulled back toward the city, leaving a rear guard before the Big Black River. On 17 May Grant's forces attacked this position, Sherman's corps overwhelming the enemy center. Many Confederates were forced into the river to swim across or drown. The remaining Southerners soon noticed that a Federal force was heading for the only bridge. Something of a footrace ensued, the Confederates reaching the bridge first while their artillery remained behind, slowing the Northerners until they were captured. As the Confederates withdrew they burned the bridge and Federal pursuit came to a halt while engineers constructed a new one.

The action at Big Black River produced one of those fortuitous moments that can affect profoundly the course of wars and of nations. As Grant was observing the battle, a messenger appeared with an order from General-in-Chief Halleck. Dated several days previous, the order directed Grant to retire without delay to Grand Gulf and then to move in support of Banks at Port Hudson. Grant and the messenger began to debate whether or not the order was still relevant: at that moment Grant heard a cheer denoting a successful charge. Exclaiming 'See that charge! I think it is too late to abandon this campaign,' he leaped onto his horse and rode toward the action. The messenger was never seen again. Had he had time to convince Grant to obey the order, Vicksburg might never have fallen.

That night the beaten Rebels marched back into town. One of the soldiers remembered: 'By nightfall the fugitive and disheveled troops were pouring into the streets of Vicksburg, and the citizens beheld with dismay the army that had gone out to fight for their safety returning to them in the character of a wild, tumultuous and mutinous mob.' On 18 May Johnston notified Richmond that defense of the city was hopeless. Grant meanwhile sent a detachment to keep Johnston at bay. Thus Pemberton was bottled up and Johnston helpless.

While his army moved across the new bridge on 18 May, Grant and Sherman stood surveying the defenses of Vicksburg, the goal of so many months of complex and frustrating campaigning. Sherman observed that up to this moment he had been unsure of their ultimate success, and added generously that

it was the end of one of the greatest campaigns in military history.

Sherman was right enough, except for the fact that Vicksburg itself was not yet conquered. To be sure, it would take a miracle to save it – but the South had been known to produce miracles. The fortifications around Vicksburg had been seven months in the making. They comprised a line nine miles long, with nine forts as strong points. The works took advantage of the broken ground around the city, which made it an excellent place to defend and a dangerous one to attack. Restless at the idea of a protracted siege, Grant attempted an assault on 19 May, resulting only in a few yards' gain toward the

Top: A Union position during the siege of Vicksburg.
Above: The flagship *Benton* leads Federal gunboats and transports in the dash past the bluffs.

city. Another assault was mounted on the afternoon of the 22nd: it proved a costly failure. The 13,000 Confederate defenders turned back 35,000 Federals and inflicted 3200 casualties; Southern casualties were around 500. (Grant was later to write that he regretted this assault, as well as a later and more disastrous one at Cold Harbor in 1864.) Within Vicksburg, the spirits of Pemberton's men revived in the aftermath of their success.

Grant then settled into a siege, gradually extending his lines over fifteen miles in a bear-hug around Vicksburg. Federal supplies and reinforcements arrived steadily until the Northerners numbered some 71,000. Washington co-operated fully: as Halleck wrote to Lincoln, 'To open the Mississippi River would be better than the capture of forty Richmonds.'

The opposing lines were at times only a few yards apart; soldiers of the two sides regularly exchanged news and gibes. Sharpshooters picked off anyone careless enough to poke his head above the ramparts. On 25 June and 1 July Federal mines under the defenses were blown up, but the planned attacks did not develop.

Within the city the civilians dug into the hills to escape incessant shelling from Union batteries and gunboats. Citizens and soldiers starved together: by late June most of the army's mules had been consumed. One soldier recalled that he and his companions came positively to enjoy a hearty helping of fried rat for breakfast – indeed, by the end of the siege rats were something of an endangered species in the city. On the Federal side, in mid-June the staff was outraged by a letter written to the press by McClernand, which implied that he and his corps were largely responsible for the campaign's success. Grant dismissed McClernand forthwith.

A major Federal assault on the starving garrison was planned for 6 July, but on the 3rd, as the Southern high-water in the East was breaking in distant

The US gunboats *De Kalb*, *Mound City* and *Cincinnati* of the Mississippi Fleet.

Gettysburg, white flags appeared on the ramparts of Vicksburg. Union troops danced, cheered and set off cannon. Soon Pemberton, an old army acquaintance of Grant, appeared, and Grant asked of him the same unconditional surrender he had demanded at Fort Donelson. When Pemberton curtly declined these terms, Grant hastened to negotiate. While the generals of the opposing staffs discussed terms, Grant and Pemberton sat on a hillside frostily passing the time of day. After some discussion Pemberton agreed to surrender the garrison on 4 July, Independence Day, and Grant agreed to parole the Confederates rather than imprison them. (To this point in the war, prisoners of both sides were often paroled until exchanged.)

At three o'clock in the afternoon of 4 July 1863, 30,000 ragged and hungry Confederates filed out of Vicksburg to stack their arms. Union troops watched in silence: as he would in future victories, Grant forbade any demonstration of triumph by his troops (though one unit was heard to cheer the valor of the Confederates). Federals were seen reaching into their supplies to give food to the Rebels.

To the north, at Gettysburg, the South had just lost a great battle. But here in Vicksburg the Confederacy had, in effect, already lost the war. Port Hudson, the last Confederate stronghold on the river, fell to Banks on 8 July. The South was shattered in two, the Mississippi lay open to the North. In Washington a jubilant Lincoln wrote 'The Father of Waters runs unvexed to the sea.'

Grant had carried off one of the greatest campaigns in history, showing his gift for wide-ranging strategic planning that took advantage of the North's superiority in materiel and manpower, and based more on maneuver than on fighting. Grant was soon to pit his strategic brilliance against the tactical genius on the battlefield of Robert E Lee: then the war would become a duel of strategy versus tactics, of Northern industrial might pitted against Southern fighting spirit and resourcefulness.

Turret of the USS *Monitor* pock-marked by shells after an 1862 naval engagement.

CHAPTER SIX
THE WAR AFLOAT
FROM IRONCLADS TO THE ALABAMA

AT THE BEGINNING OF the Civil War the belligerent sides made haste to begin building navies. The North then possessed 90 ships of all classes, but only 41 were in commission and half those were obsolete sailing ships in an age of steam. The Confederacy quite simply had no navy at the outset, though it did possess an abundant supply of experienced naval officers who had cast their lot with home states in the South.

Overseeing the Union fleet was Secretary of the Navy Gideon Welles, who came to the job relatively inexperienced but soon generated an extraordinary burst of naval production. Firmly managing the conflicting pressures of politics and practicality, Welles proved to be one of the most able Cabinet officers in history. His opposite in the Confederacy was Stephen R Mallory, who before joining the South-

Previous spread: The history-making battle of the ironclads USS *Monitor* and *Merrimac* (CSS *Virginia*) 9 March 1862.
Right: CSS *Alabama* burns a prize.
Below: A pontoon bridge across the James River, typical of those used during the war for troop movement, supply and evacuation.

ern cause had been chairman of the Senate Naval Affairs Committee, where he had been instrumental in modernizing the US fleet. Since the South lagged dramatically behind the North in industrial capacity and lacked shipbuilding facilities almost entirely, Mallory began purchasing ships from abroad and from private owners, developing from nothing a Confederate Navy of imposing effectiveness. Unlike Welles, Mallory was quick to seize on new ideas, one of which – ironclad ships – would bring about a revolution in naval warfare. (Mallory also experimented with submarines, but in the long run these proved more dangerous to their crews than to Union shipping.)

The Federal Navy's first major challenge came directly after the surrender of Fort Sumter, when President Lincoln proclaimed a blockade of Southern ports. To enforce the blockade across 3500 miles of Southern coastline seemed at first a hopeless task, but Welles assembled a motley fleet of mercantile vessels that immediately put a small but significant dent in Southern shipping. Meanwhile, Union shipyards began constructing a fleet specifically designed for the blockade. To counter this the South had built a fleet of blockade-runners – fast, sleek steamships painted black and burning smokeless coal, capable of running unseen in the night past Federal blockaders. Thereby Southern shipping went on: cotton out, arms and supplies in. But the Union net squeezed ever tighter.

THE BATTLE OF IRONCLADS

In early 1861 Secretary Mallory had already given priority to constructing an iron-armored battleship for the Confederacy. There were then only two such vessels in the world, one French, the other British: they had recently demonstrated their effectiveness against Russian forts. Mallory's plans were unwittingly aided by the Union when in April 1861 the Federals hastily abandoned the navy yard in Norfolk, Virginia, leaving to the South vast stores of munitions and a half-burned steam frigate. This ship, the USS *Merrimac*, was salvaged by the Confederates with the hull intact and rebuilt as an ironclad ram, rechristened the CSS *Virginia* (though history would persist in calling it the *Merrimac*). Shipbuilder John L Porter designed for the boat a citadel to contain four rifled guns and six smoothbores. The sloping sides were built up from 22 inches of oak topped by four inches of railroad iron greased with tallow. The resulting armored citadel made up 170 feet of the 260-foot-long ship. A cast-iron ramming prow projected four feet from the bow. Sailing with its decks awash, the rebuilt *Merrimac* looked rather like a floating barn roof.

News of its construction had made its way to the North, and the Navy Department immediately initiated its own development of ironclads. In early August 1861 Congress allocated money for the purpose, and the construction race began. Among

Top: An engraving of the USS *Monitor* published in 1862.
Above: The Federal Navy's bombardment of Fort Walker, Port Royal Harbor, South Carolina, in the first years of the war.
Left: The Battle of the Ironclads as depicted by American painter William Torgerson.

A smoothbore Dahlgren gun that fired a spherical shell, typical of the armament of Confederate gunboats.

three prototype ironclad projects, the most innovative was that of John Ericsson, a Swedish-born engineer. The foundation of his design was a hull flat on top and covered with iron plates, rising only a couple of feet above the water. Projecting from this iron raft were a stubby pilothouse in front, a short smokestack to the rear, and in the middle a heavily armored rotating iron turret some nine feet high and weighing 140 tons. Although the turret was armed with only two large smoothbore cannon, the rotating feature enabled it to shoot in almost any direction.

The revolutionary design – containing upward of 40 patentable ideas – and eccentric appearance of this prototype, christened the *Monitor*, caused a good deal of snide comment: it was called an 'iron pot,' a 'cheesebox on a raft,' 'Ericsson's Folly.' More seriously, there were grave doubts within the Navy Department about the viability of the ship, as well as the sanity of its inventor. Accordingly, Captain

(soon to be Admiral) David Dixon Porter was dispatched to look over the *Monitor* as it neared completion. Designer Ericsson proved to be as eccentric as his ship, and Porter was subjected to a withering barrage of queries designed to prove the captain's ignorance of higher mathematics. Shown a model of the vessel, Porter failed to reassure Ericsson when he examined it upside down. But as he toured the interior of the ship, Porter the practical navy man was able to recognize something extraordinary when he saw it; after his examination he told Ericsson it was 'the most remarkable vessel the world has ever seen – one that, if properly handled, can destroy any ship now afloat and whip a dozen wooden ships together.' A suddenly delighted Ericsson exclaimed 'My God! And all this time I took you for a damned fool!'

In the end the *Monitor* was completed in remarkably short time: her keel laid on 25 October 1861, she was launched on 30 January 1862, captained by

Lieutenant Lorimer Worden. After fitting out she
sailed on 6 March from New York toward Hampton
Roads, Virginia, on Chesapeake Bay near Norfolk.
It was not a moment too soon. The Union Navy had
so far managed to dominate that part of the Virginia
coast, to isolate Norfolk and generally to tighten the
blockade. But on 8 March the *Merrimac*, under
Captain Franklin S Buchanan, steamed out to
Hampton Roads to drive away the blockading ships.

As the *Merrimac* lumbered into view, the Federals
knew her at sight: she had been expected for weeks,
and they were ready for her. Or so they thought. The
Merrimac made directly for the 30-gun frigate
Cumberland; the 50-gun USS *Congress* meanwhile
unleashed a massive broadside on the Rebel ironclad. Soon the *Merrimac* was under fire from both
Federal ships and the shore. To the Northerners'
dismay, this terrific barrage had no effect whatever:
the shot bounced off the ironclad like marbles off a
brick wall. The *Merrimac* rammed directly into the
Cumberland, breaking off the ironclad's beak but
opening a gaping hole in the Federal ship. The
Cumberland began to sink while the *Merrimac*
peppered her with shell. Meanwhile, accompanying
Confederate ships opened fire on the *Congress*, to
great effect. Suffering heavy casualties and in
flames, the *Congress* surrendered. While trying to
help, three Union steam frigates ran aground.

It had been a devastatingly one-sided battle. The
Merrimac retired without serious damage at five
o'clock in the afternoon. Confederate Captain

Buchanan had been injured, and Lieutenant
Catesby ap Roger Jones took over command of the
Merrimac. The Rebel sailors looked forward to an
easy destruction of the Federal fleet on the following
day.

News of the battle brought consternation to
Washington next morning, 9 March. The President
chaired a tumultuous Cabinet meeting: Secretary of
War Stanton paced the floor in a panic, proclaim-
ing: 'Likely her first move will be to come up the
Potomac and disperse Congress, destroy the Capitol

Above: The sinking of
the USS *Cumberland*, 8
March 1862.
Below: The Battle of the
Ironclads in Hampton
Roads, as seen from the
shoreline.

the Confederates took it for a boiler going for repairs on a raft; its first shot, about nine in the morning, was thought to be an accidental explosion on the raft. It was, of course, the *Monitor*, and she was arriving in the very nick of time. The world's first battle of ironclads, the beginning of the modern naval age, had begun.

The two ships closed in, firing constantly, until they were occasionally touching. Several times the *Merrimac* tried to ram the *Monitor*, but the smaller ship easily outmaneuvered her enemy – the underpowered Confederate ironclad could only make five knots and required half an hour to turn around. Both ships probed with their guns, trying without success to find a weak spot on their opponent. The *Monitor*'s turret swung toward the enemy to fire, away to load. Gunners inside several times came close to shelling their own pilothouse, and made note that future monitors should have the pilothouse on top of the turret. In the first two hours of fighting, the *Monitor* was hit 21 times without serious damage; likewise, the nearly point-blank Federal firing was able to crack but not to penetrate the *Merrimac*'s armor.

Inside the boats the crews were relatively protected, but by no means comfortable. Temperatures inside the *Monitor*'s turret soared over 170 degrees; concussions from enemy shot sent screwheads, with which the armor was secured to bolts, flying around the interior; and the din was almost unbearable. Inside the *Merrimac* 21 crew members were wounded in the course of battle, though none seriously.

After both ships had given it their best, the battle

Above: The wreck of the *Monitor* in a gale off Cape Hatteras.
Below: Sketch plans of Monitor-class ships of the post-Civil War period.
Opposite: A young 'powder monkey,' employed to carry powder to the guns.

and public buildings. . . . Not unlikely we shall have a shell in the White House before we leave this room.' Lincoln ran anxiously to the window to search the Potomac for the approach of the *Merrimac*.

That same morning the *Merrimac* steamed out to battle at Hampton Roads. But as the ironclad headed for the Federal ships, Rebels in her saw a strange object slip around the bow of the grounded USS *Minnesota* and head directly for them. At first

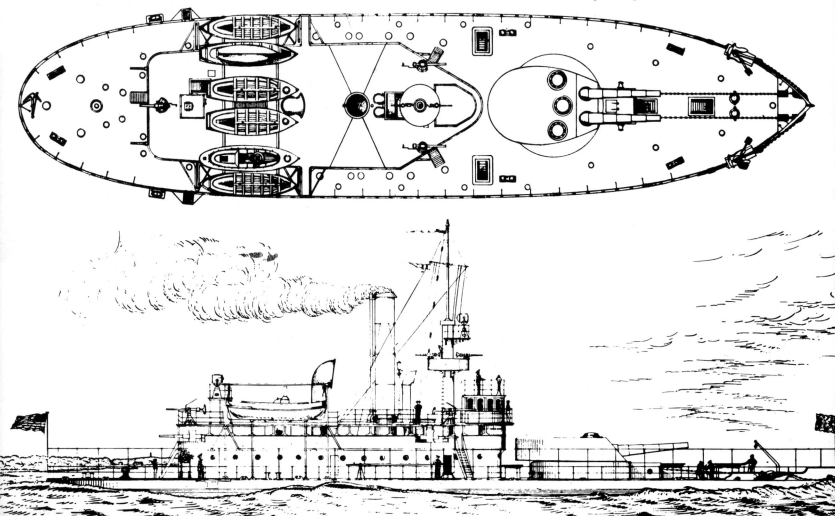

trailed off indecisively after noon. The *Merrimac* withdrew, leaking steadily; her parting shot hit the *Monitor*'s pilothouse, temporarily blinding Captain Worden. Several times over the next few days the *Merrimac* steamed out to challenge the *Monitor*, but

Far Right: Captain Raphael Semmes aboard the Southern commerce raider *Alabama.*

Right: Interior of the *Monitor*'s turret, where oven-like temperatures and flying metal bolts endangered crewmen in battle.
Below: Crew members of the USS *Monitor* relax and prepare a meal on deck.

the Union ship was ordered not to risk an engagement: she had amply served her purpose and saved the Federal fleet.

Ironically, both the *Monitor* and the *Merrimac* were soon to perish outside of battle. In May 1862 the Confederates abandoned Norfolk; with her excessive 22 feet of draft and her unseaworthiness, the *Merrimac* could neither sail up the James to Richmond nor move to another base. Reluctantly, the Confederates burned and scuttled her. The almost equally unseaworthy *Monitor* was swamped in a gale off Cape Hatteras in December 1862. (In October 1983, solid remains of the *Monitor* were located by underwater archaeologists.)

But despite their stalemate, both ships had amply proved their point. A new era had arrived: governments around the world were forced to realize their fleets were obsolete. And the North and South began building more ironclads at top speed, each on the model of its first vessel.

RUNNING THE BLOCKADE

From 1861 on the Federal blockade of the South operated with increasing success. In effect, the whole Confederacy was under siege by Union ships, and vital imports of food, clothing and armaments were slowly but inexorably choked off. Evading the blockade was a necessity for Southern survival, and at first the Confederacy was notably successful at it. Over the course of the war, some 8250 of the sleek, fast, blockade-running ships were in use and brought in goods valued at over $200 million, including most of the small arms used by the Confederate Army. In addition to its own vessels, the Confederate Government required English ships running the blockade to carry arms and supplies as well as consumer goods.

Blockade-running proved a highly profitable business for adventurers willing to pursue it. Fortunes could be made in a voyage or two – a profit of $300,000 on a round trip was not uncommon. Much of this profit was made on luxury goods – silks, satins and jewelry often vied with guns for space on board. (In 1864, when the South was in desperate straits, President Davis finally put a stop to the luxury traffic.) The usual route for cargo was from England or Europe to the Bahamas. There the goods were transferred to blockade-runners for the dash

Below: A moonlit anchorage in Pamlico Sound near Roanoke Island.

The *Alabama* in battle, 19 June 1864.

into port on the mainland. Southern cotton exports went out by the reverse route. Two Southern seamen later recalled those dangerous journeys:

Amidst almost impenetrable darkness, without lightship or beacon, the narrow and close watched inlet was felt for with a deep-sea lead as a blind man feels his way along a familiar path, and even when the enemy's fire was raking the wheelhouse, the faithful pilot, with steady hand and iron nerve, safely steered the little fugitive of the sea to her desired haven. He could not get his bearings on the darkest night by a taste of the land. The men who ran the blockade had to be men who could stand fire without returning it. It was a business in which every man took his life in his hands. . . . He who made a success of it was obliged to have the cunning of a fox, the patience of a Job, and the bravery of a Spartan warrior.

In 1861 the chance of capture for blockade-runners was about one in ten. By 1864, with some 600 Federal ships patroling the coast, the chance had risen to one in three, and the pinch on Southern supplies had become fatal. Perhaps as much as any other single element of its strategy, the Union's blockade finally ensured the defeat of the South.

THE BATTLE OF NEW ORLEANS

One by one the Union conquered the vital Confederate ports. Among the most important was that of New Orleans, the gateway to the Mississippi River Valley and the largest city of the Confederacy. In November 1861 Union Admiral David Glasgow Farragut, age 61, was given the task of leading a naval assault on the city.

The defenses of New Orleans were formidable: two masonry forts, Jackson and St Philip, faced one another on opposite banks of the Mississippi below the city; from their walls some 80 guns were trained on the river. However, the Confederate commander of the city, Mansfield Lovell, was too sanguine about his defenses. Apparently fooled by a Federal diversion near Pensacola, Florida, he reported nearby Union troop concentrations as 'harmless' and failed to repair storm damage to a chain barricade across the river, an important part of his defenses.

On 18 April 1862 Farragut opened a bombardment on the Rebel forts, using 13-inch shells from mortars in specially converted boats. For a week the Federals sent hundreds of shells a day into the forts, but Farragut finally had to admit they were having no great effect on the Rebel batteries, and the Union ships would have to go in under full enemy fire. At two in the morning on 24 April Farragut, on his flagship *Hartford*, began sending his ships upriver past the Confederate forts. Alerted by the sound of the Federal ships raising anchor, the Rebel gunners opened up. As Union vessels opened their guns in reply, it seemed to one participant as if 'all the earthquakes in the world and all the thunder and lightnings were going off at once.' Enemy gunboats, including the ironclad *Louisiana* and the cigar-shaped ironclad ram *Manassas*, sailed out to the attack. Above the river shells flashed and crashed like the day of judgment; on the ships it was bright as day, but the smoke made the distance impenetrable. A tugboat pushing a fire-raft bore down on the *Hartford*, setting it aflame: Farragut cooly advised his gunners, 'There's a hotter fire than that for those who don't do their duty.' The *Hartford* never ceased firing while the flames were being stopped. But the Federal fleet passed the forts with surprisingly little damage (36 killed and 135 wounded) and proceeded on to engage the Confederate fleet before New Orleans. In the fight only one Federal vessel was lost – the converted merchantman *Varuna*, first struck at close range by the Confederate *Governor Moore* firing downward through its own bow, then fatally rammed by the *Stonewall Jackson*.

The Confederate fleet finally destroyed, New Orleans was captured next day, 25 April. On 29 April the Rebel defenders in the forts mutinied and forced their commanders to surrender. One of the great Southern cities had fallen: now the path to Vicksburg on the Mississippi was largely open.

Left: The Palmetto Battery at Charleston, South Carolina, in 1863.
Below: The swift Confederate blockade-runner *A D Vance*, captured by the Union Navy in the course of the war and refitted for its service.

THE BATTLE OF MOBILE BAY

Having commanded the expedition that closed the port of New Orleans in 1862, it was again the elderly but indefatigable and hard-fighting Farragut who, in the fiercest naval battle of the war, closed down one of the last remaining Confederate ports at Mobile Bay, Alabama, in August of 1864. Farragut's opponent in Mobile was Franklin S Buchanan, former captain of the *Merrimac*. The Confederates had covered the harbor with obstacles including a number of 'moored torpedoes' – later to be called mines. The Rebel fleet in Mobile Bay boasted a new ironclad, the CSS *Tennessee*, of the *Merrimac* design, and three wooden gunboats.

In the early morning of 5 August 1864, Farragut on his flagship *Hartford* led a Union fleet into the narrow entrance of Mobile Bay. He had with him four turreted ironclads of the *Monitor* class and fourteen wooden ships, which were lashed together in pairs. Along with the Southern gunboats, Confederate forts on both sides of the entrance opened deadly fire on the oncoming Federals, 'mowing down the men, deluging the decks with blood, and scattering mangled fragments of humanity so thickly that it was difficult to stand on the deck.'

As Farragut pushed into the harbor in the face of this cannonade, disaster struck one of his ironclads: just before eight o'clock the *Tecumseh* hit a moored torpedo and quickly sank with nearly all hands. It was then that Farragut reportedly shouted his legendary words of defiance, 'Damn the torpedoes! Full speed ahead!' In any case, that is what the Union fleet did. Though the sailors could hear torpedoes scraping along the bottoms of their ships, no more exploded. But as they moved into the harbor, the fleet faced a new threat – the Confederate ironclad ram *Tennessee* moved out to the attack around eight o'clock. Nothing daunted, Farragut, lashed high in the rigging to oversee the course of battle, opened fire and ordered the *Hartford* and two other ships to ram the *Tennessee* at five-minute intervals. Federal gunboats hammered the slow-moving ironclad relentlessly for over an hour. Becoming unable to fire due to defective fuses, the *Tennessee* foundered out of control and finally surrendered at about ten o'clock. Meanwhile, Confederate commander Buchanan had been incapacitated by a broken leg.

At that point the Confederates conceded the bay to the North. It was another 16 days before Rebel forts fell to ground troops, and the city of Mobile itself remained unconquered until the end of the war. The cost of the battle in Mobile Bay was high for a naval engagement in the war – the North had 319 casualties (including 93 drowned in the *Tecumseh*), the South lost 312 (including 280 captured). But one of the last leaks in the Union blockade had been stopped.

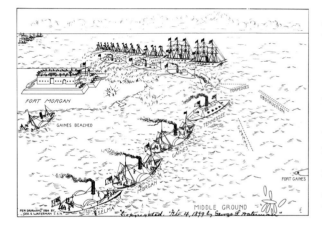

Right: The Battle of Mobile Bay, as depicted by George S Waterman, CSN.
Below: Surrender of CSS *Tennessee* at Mobile Bay, 5 August 1864, in the last major naval engagement of the war.

DUEL AT CHERBOURG

Soon after the outbreak of war the Confederacy began sending ships to raid Union seagoing commerce around the world. Some of these ships were converted Southern private vessels, others were purchased abroad. Among the latter was the steam sloop *Alabama*, bought during its construction in England early in 1862. Under Captain Raphael Semmes, the *Alabama* set out on a two-year campaign of commerce raiding that accounted for some 58 prizes and $6,547,000 in losses to Union shipping.

Lacking heavy armament – one rifled 6.4-inch gun, a 68-pound shell gun and six 32-pound smoothbores – the *Alabama* relied on stealth and surprise for its success, often approaching her prey under a Union flag. Semmes quickly became a feared and almost legendary marauder of the high seas.

On 11 June 1864, the *Alabama* entered the harbor of Cherbourg, France, for some much-needed repairs. Three days later the Federal steam sloop *Kearsarge*, captained by John A Winslow, appeared in the harbor. Winslow contacted Semmes and asked him to release to the *Kearsarge* some Federal prisoners held on the Confederate ship. In response, Semmes sent a challenge: though his ship was partly disabled and his opponent superior in armament, speed and number of crew, Semmes confidently challenged the *Kearsarge* to battle. Winslow was happy to oblige. The date agreed to was 19 June.

News of the coming duel seemed to travel around Europe like lightning. When the *Alabama* steamed out of harbor to meet the waiting *Kearsarge* on the appointed day, the bluffs of Cherbourg were bustling with spectators, the water bristling with ships, including the British yacht *Deerhound* and a French fleet. A band on one of the French ships serenaded the Confederates with Southern melodies as the *Alabama* sailed past, polished to the nines and with her crew dressed as though for review.

The ships closed to a mile's distance, whence the *Alabama* fired the first broadside at about 11:00 AM. The *Kearsarge* replied, and the guns roared steadily as the duelling ships circled closer. After some 15 minutes the Confederates lodged a percussion shell in the Federal vessel. The shell failed to explode, and as the *Kearsarge* closed to point-blank range the Confederate crew realized how much more maneuverable their opponent was. Soon they learned that the Federals were also much the superior gunners.

The *Alabama*, in fact, was being shot to pieces: the bulwarks disappeared, guns were disabled, compartments below had their partitions shot away and response at the helm became dull. Finally, a shell penetrated the *Alabama* at waterline and exploded in the engine room, shaking the whole vessel. It was the final blow. His ship sinking fast and 40 of his crew dead or disabled, Semmes hoisted the white flag. As the *Kearsarge* pulled away to watch,

Above: The 11-inch forward pivot gun in action on the *Kearsarge*.

some Confederate sailors boarded the remaining boats and others leaped overboard. The latter group included the gallant but overconfident Semmes, who dropped his sword over the side before following it. Union losses were one killed and two wounded. The British *Deerhound* closed in to pick up Semmes and the other Rebel survivors, and sailors of both sides joined the hundreds of spectators in watching the *Alabama* slide majestically under the waves.

The sinking of the *Alabama* was actually one of the smaller defeats in that year of defeat for the South, but the old-fashioned and perhaps ill-advised gallantry of the Rebels falling before the inexorable might of Union fighting power was a microcosm of the whole war, and the battle was one of the legends of its time.

Left: The sinking of the redoubtable *Alabama* off Cherbourg, France, 19 June 1864.
Below left: The USS *Cairo*.
Below: Captain Raphael Semmes of the steam sloop *Alabama*, most successful of the Southern commerce raiders.

The Battle of
Gettysburg, scene of the
highest casualties of the
Civil War.

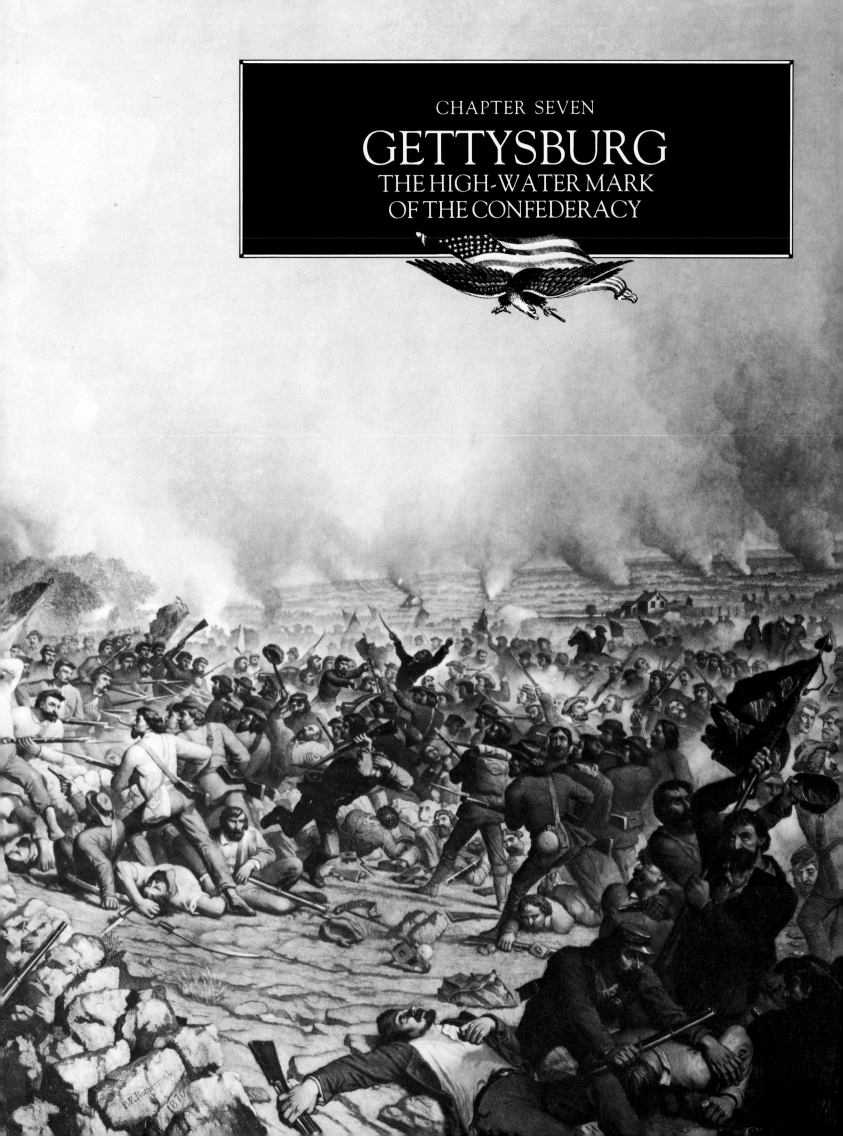

CHAPTER SEVEN
GETTYSBURG
THE HIGH-WATER MARK
OF THE CONFEDERACY

BATTLES ARE FOUGHT by men, behind whose doings are passions, convictions and uncertainties. Men fight as members of armies, and behind their operations – victories, defeats, and the profound comradeship borne of shared suffering – is the vast and devious machinery of nations, of politics and money. In June of 1863 the two great armies of the East were on the march, moving inexorably toward the convulsion that everyone knew had to come some time, and which both sides fervently prayed would settle everything once and for all.

The Confederate Army of Northern Virginia marched ragged and hungry, as always. The Confederacy lacked money to keep them up properly, though neither Lee nor his government had the patience to organize supply lines as well as they could have – the South at that point had enough at least to feed the army better than they were fed. The men were hungry, many lacked shoes and most wore rags. Still, they had whipped the well-fed and superbly outfitted Yankees three times in the past year – at the Second Bull Run, Fredericksburg and Chancellorsville, with Antietam more or less a draw – and they were led by the greatest general in the world. If ever an army felt invincible, the Army of

General James Longstreet, whom Lee called 'my old warhorse,' commanded I Corps at Gettysburg.

Northern Virginia did that summer. And now they were headed toward Washington.

But things were not so good as they seemed for the South. Lee's decision to invade the North for the second time was made partly in desperation. The situation in the Confederacy was critical: the Mississippi was all but lost; badly needed European recognition had not come; the Union blockade was tightening; anti-war sentiment in the North was fading; Southern finances were collapsing. The only hope for the Confederacy now, Lee reasoned, was a decisive victory that would win the war in one stroke. On the desk of Jefferson Davis was a letter to be given to Lincoln after that victory: a letter from the victor to the vanquished, proposing terms for peace.

Lee knew his army would follow him anywhere, and he believed they could whip anybody – their string of victories proved it. At 57 he was getting to be an old man; his heart was beginning to trouble him, and he did not know how many battles he or the Confederacy had left. He must act *now*. But his convictions were not shared by his second in command, James Longstreet, whom Lee affectionately called 'my old war horse.' Longstreet objected to the invasion from the beginning, proposing instead a plan to hold Hooker and his Union Army of the Potomac with two divisions while sending the rest to Tennessee, where they would join Bragg and Johnston in fighting Rosecrans. This move would probably force Grant away from his siege of Vicksburg, paralyze the North and threaten Kentucky and Ohio.

It was a good plan and might very well have worked, but Lee rejected it. His sights, as always, were fixed above all on his beloved Virginia: he wanted to end the Union threat to his exhausted state and find food for his army in the farms of Pennsylvania. The most Longstreet could get from Lee was agreement that the campaign should be offensive in strategy but defensive in tactics. And in the end Lee would not abide by that notion either. Two men: their passion for their cause coincided, but their convictions diverged, and diverged fatally.

Lee's first move was to reorganize his army into three corps with integral artillery: those led by Longstreet, A P Hill, and – replacing Stonewall Jackson as best he could – the brilliant and eccentric Richard S Ewell. Added to this was an oversize cavalry division under Jeb Stuart – in all, some 89,000 men.

The Confederate Army pulled out of its old field of triumph, Fredericksburg, Virginia, on 3 June, leaving Hill behind to fool Hooker and the Army of the Potomac. But Joe Hooker was not to be fooled this time. Union reconnaissance parties skirmished with the Rebels at Franklin's Crossing (5 June) and Brandy Station (8 June) and established that Lee was on the march. Concentrating around Culpeper, Virginia, Lee sent Ewell to clear away R H Milroy's Federals in the Shenandoah Valley, which was accomplished easily enough. It was hoped this operation would keep Hooker away from Richmond

and put him in a defensive posture. It did just that. The state militias of Maryland and Pennsylvania hastened to organize against Lee, but their resistance was pathetically inadequate. So far, then, things were not going badly for the campaign.

By mid-June Hill had left Fredericksburg, and the whole Army of Northern Virginia was on the move through Maryland to the northwest, circling Washington. Paralleling them to the east like a shadow were Hooker and the Army of the Potomac, 122,000 strong, staying between the Rebel Army and Washington. Hooker entreated his superiors to let him march on Richmond, but General-in-Chief Henry Halleck insisted on maintaining a defensive posture. Meanwhile, Halleck was trying to find some way to get around Hooker's political supporters and give the army to someone else – Hooker's humiliation at Chancellorsville was not to be overlooked.

As the South's and North's main forces marched northwest, the two cavalries, both on reconnaissance, fought a running series of skirmishes. Now the Federal horsemen (under General Alfred Pleasonton) had enough confidence and experience to challenge Jeb Stuart. Though largely indecisive, these skirmishes served to keep the Rebel cavalry at a distance from the Federal infantry: as a result, Stuart was not at all sure where the bulk of the enemy was.

This problem was soon compounded when Stuart proposed to Lee that his men repeat an old ploy of theirs – riding completely around the Federal Army. Lee agreed to the plan. Stuart set out on what seemed like a good bit of fun, but soon found he was getting more than he had bargained for. The Federals were spread out far more widely than expected; to avoid them Stuart had to detour farther and farther east. He was ultimately to be out of touch with Lee for ten days and did not rejoin the army until the second night of the battle. The effect on Lee's campaign was devastating – the Confederate Army was in effect marching blindfolded into enemy territory.

Thus Lee moved into Pennsylvania, his forces widely separated, not knowing that Hooker had crossed the Potomac (15-16 June), and that the Federal Army was squarely on the Confederate flank and the shortest road to Richmond. Finally, on 28 June, a spy revealed to Lee that the Federals were concentrating around Frederick, Maryland; moreover, the Army of the Potomac had a new commander. In late June Hooker had ordered the XII Corps to join the Federal garrison at Harper's Ferry and operate on the rear of Lee's army. Halleck countermanded the order and, as was hoped, this blow to his authority was too much for Hooker. He resigned on 28 June and was replaced by General George G Meade, who despite his protests was chosen over his superior John Reynolds and ordered to command virtually on the eve of battle.

It was the fifth change of command in ten months

The invasion of Pennsylvania: Columbia Railroad Bridge at Wrightsville burning in background.

General George Meade and staff at headquarters after the Battle of Gettysburg.

for the Army of the Potomac, and a good sign of how desperate the authorities in Washington were. By now the soldiers scarcely cared any more: they had long since lost enthusiasm for the whole race of generals, and most of them knew little of Meade. He was a drawn and gloomy man, still suffering from the effects of a wound at White Oak Swamp, and his foul temper was legendary among his subordinates. The terrible burden of responsibilty that dropped on him so unexpectedly served only to make Meade still more gloomy and irascible. But if not truly brilliant, Meade was still a tough and competent general. Hearing the news, Lee prophesied accurately 'General Meade will make no blunder on my front.' Meade's army consisted by now of seasoned, hardened soldiers. Cynical as they had become about commanders, they were ready to do as they were told. They had seen victory elude their grasp time and time again and knew it was not their fault; they were ready to win if only they could find a leader who would let them. Realizing the enemy was on his flank, Lee decided to concentrate at the nearest place handy, which happened to be Gettysburg, Pennsylvania, a little town with a great many road crossings. Lee was by no means planning a battle there: he could not in any case, for with Stuart

gone he was still unsure just where the Army of the Potomac was. He was concentrating simply in order to discourage operations on the rear of his army. If it came to battle his intended position was to be nearby Cashtown, which would be ideal for defense.

Meade, however, had made the same decision – to concentrate at Gettysburg – and for the same reason: convenience. Like Lee, he was not entirely certain where his enemy was. His real goal was to settle into a defensive position at Pipe Creek, 15 miles southeast of Gettysburg. Thus the most terrible battle ever fought on American soil was about to break out by accident. The course of the battle would also be significantly determined by happenstance – the Confederate Army was by then fairly tightly concentrated, the Union Army spread out. Jeb Stuart was still skylarking, Lee still blindfolded and A P Hill's men had heard they might find some shoes in town.

On 1 July John Buford's Federal cavalry division was scouting in Gettysburg. Buford, a tough old cavalry soldier, had felt a premonition they would run into trouble. Watching from a ridge just west of town that morning, Buford saw the trouble coming: a column of enemy troops, preceded by skirmishers, slogging toward town. They were Harry Heth's division of Hill's corps, and they were looking for shoes, not Yankees.

The 2500 Federal cavalry dismounted, formed a thin line of battle from McPherson's Ridge north to Seminary Ridge and began firing away with their new Spencer repeating carbines. The Rebels spread out and returned fire. By ten in the morning the fighting was hot and Confederates seemed to be pouring in from everywhere. General William D Pender had arrived to support Heth, and Federal cavalrymen were now badly outnumbered, but still they held on. Buford had sent a plea for help to John Reynolds and the I Corps. About ten o'clock in the morning Reynolds arrived just in front of his corps, expertly surveyed the situation and rushed to position his arriving infantry. They included John Gibbon's old bunch, the black-hatted Iron Brigade, a legendary outfit since their first battle at the Second Bull Run. (They were now under Solomon J Merideth.) As they fell into line the Iron Brigade could hear the Rebels observing 'Here are those damned black-hat fellers agin. . . . 'Tain't no militia – that's the Army of the Potomac!'

Hill's Confederates were now falling into line in waves. The I Corps took over from the exhausted cavalrymen and began to stabilize the Union position a little. General Abner Doubleday captured his old friend General James Archer and a large part of his brigade (Archer was the first of Lee's general officers ever to be captured). The Federals were slowly pushed back from McPherson's Ridge to Seminary Ridge, but they were not in retreat. Hundreds of Southerners were captured after vicious fighting in a railroad cut to the South. General Reynolds rode behind his lines, strengthening the position. He was considered by many the best soldier

High Tide at Gettysburg by Charles S Reinhart captures the ferocity of this epic struggle.

in the Union Army, the man who should have been commander of the Army of the Potomac all along. But a sharpshooter's bullet knocked Reynolds dead from his saddle early in the action. Without a commander now, his men held the line.

At noon there was an ominous lull. Heth formed his Confederates south of the Cashtown road. Federal Generals Abner Doubleday and James Wadsworth dressed their lines along and in front of Seminary Ridge as the rest of the I Corps arrived and fell into line. About 1:00 PM Oliver O Howard's XI Corps, called forward urgently, began arriving; the divisions of Carl Shurz and Francis Barlow took position to the north, on the Federal right. Howard decided to leave an artillery reserve on Cemetery Hill, just south of town. His placement of the battery on Cemetery Hill turned out to be one of those small decisions that win battles, for the Union was about to need that position desperately. Lee by early afternoon had decided to throw everything he had at the Federals. Ewell, leading Jackson's old corps, descended from the north onto the Federal right. The still luckless XI Corps were flanked as they had been at Chancellorsville and finally caved in, with Barlow critically wounded. Frantic calls went back to the nearest Union corps, Daniel E Sickles's (III) and Henry W Slocum's (XII). The XI Corps fled through Gettysburg and there in the streets ran into large masses of Rebels.

The collapse of the XI Corps in the north made the position of Doubleday, now commanding the I Corps, untenable to the south. Things heated up quickly; as a Federal cannoneer remembered the ensuing struggle:

The enemy . . . made his appearance in grand shape. His line stretched nearly a mile in length. First we could see the tips of their color staffs coming up over the little ridge, then the points of their bayonets, and then the Johnnies themselves, coming on with a steady tramp, tramp, and with loud yells. In quick, sharp tones, like successive reports of a repeating rifle, came our captain's orders: 'Load . . . Canister . . . Double!'

Directly in our front the Rebel infantry had been forced to halt and lie down, by the tornado of canister that we had given them. But the regiments to their right kept on, as if to cut us off from the rest of our troops.

Then ensued probably the most desperate fight ever waged between artillery and infantry at close range without a particle of cover on either side. They gave us volley after volley in front and flank, and we gave them double canister as fast as we could load. . . .

Up and down the line men were reeling and falling; splinters flying from wheels and axles where bullets hit; in rear, horses tearing and plunging, drivers yelling, shells bursting, shot shrieking overhead, howling about our ears . . . the musketry crashing on three sides of us . . . smoke, dust, splinters, blood, wreck and carnage indescribable.

Finally along with most of the I Corps, what little was left of the battery was pulled back. On the left of the Union line the Iron Brigade had been ordered to hold out to the last extremity. This they did as Rebels swarmed onto them from three sides. Time and again they requested General Wadsorth to let them retreat; time and again Wadsworth refused. One stand of colors had five color-bearers shot from under the same flag, the last being the commanding general. Finally, the devastated Iron Brigade pulled back to barricades at the Seminary and made another stand before Hill pushed them back again.

The Confederates pressed on relentlessly, scattering the I Corps before them. It was an all-too-familiar story for the Army of the Potomac: Lee had massed his troops to gain local superiority and was crushing his enemy piece by piece. But there remained Howard's Union artillery reserve to the south on Cemetery Hill. As evening descended, General Winfield Scott Hancock arrived at that position. He had been sent by Meade to take charge and to survey the situation.

At first sight it was bad, very bad. From the hill Hancock saw the Federals in confused rout. The I Corps had only 2400 men left of its original 10,000. The Iron Brigade was virtually ruined; its 24th Michigan Regiment had lost 399 of 496 men. The XI Corps had 4000 captured in the wild melee as they fled through Gettysburg. There were at most 5000 men left available out of two whole corps.

Shouting and cursing, Hancock slowly rallied the stragglers around Howard's battery on Cemetery Hill. As dark came on he had a serviceable position; somehow the I and XI Corps were in line of battle again. Hancock saw that this hill was not a bad place to be, in fact might be a very good position indeed. Noticing that Culp's Hill, just to the west, might be vulnerable, Hancock sent some of the I Corps survivors over to occupy it. Another serviceable position, maybe.

Across the way Ewell was taking a good look at Cemetery Hill. Lee had asked him to assault it 'if

Longstreet's 46-gun attack at Gettysburg.

Little Round Top, secured for the Federals by the 140th New York of Sykes's V Corps.

possible.' That courteous proviso would have inspired Stonewall Jackson to move mountains. But Ewell was no Jackson, and he was plagued with an odd paralysis of will in these days. He decided not to try to take Cemetery Hill. Had he tried, American history might have been very different. That position, so vulnerable that night, was to become the foundation of the Union line.

Nonetheless, the South had clearly won the day on the first of July. It had pushed the enemy back and inflicted a terrible toll on the Union Army. A confident Lee made plans for an all-out attack as early as possible next morning; his men would walk right over the enemy, just as so many times before. Yet things were, again, less good then they seemed for the South. Lee had been drawn into battle at a time and on ground not of his own choosing. With Stuart still away, Lee did not know exactly where Meade's forces were. Jackson was gone, and Longstreet recalcitrant. The enemy was in its own territory, fighting for its own soil. And though the Union army had been forced back, they had been driven onto positions that were stronger than anyone, North or South, seemed to realize that night – except perhaps for Hancock, who surveyed the area with increasing satisfaction.

This time there were to be no uncommitted corps in the Union Army, as there had been at Antietam and Chancellorsville. Meade was cautious, too much so in the long run, but this time he was going to give it everything he had. All night and next morning he moved troops into position on high ground, the lines spreading out from Cemetery Hill. He was most worried about his right flank to the north, which Ewell had smashed before. To protect this flank the Union lines bent around the hills to the north, Slocum's XII Corps from Culp's Hill south, Howard and the XI Corps bending from the side of Culp's Hill to Cemetery Hill. Below that, the I Corps (now under General John Newton since Reynolds's death) and Hancock's II Corps stretched south along Cemetery Ridge; Daniel E Sickles's III Corps was on the left flank, from the end of Cemetery Ridge to the Round Tops. George G Sykes's V Corps was to the rear in reserve; John Sedgwick's corps was still moving up. Meade established his headquarters in a shabby farmhouse on the Taneytown Road, behind the center of his line.

Good as his ground was, however, Meade's concern for the right flank – he feared the enemy could get around it to his rear – led him to build up the right and stint the left flank, especially the Round Tops, which thus became his weak points. It was just that left flank that Lee was planning to strike, on the second day of battle. Once again, Longstreet had demurred – it seemed to him impossible to assault the enemy on those heights. Instead he proposed a strategic envelopment on the right, moving around behind the Federals and coming between them and Washington; then the Union Army would have to come down from those hills and fight it out where the Confederates wanted them.

Lee would have none of this: he would strike the Union left, around the Round Tops. If he could overrun these positions he would roll up the Federal line like a rug. The Confederate Army was then stretched around the fishhook shape of Meade's lines: Ewell on the left with the divisions of Johnson, Early and Rodes; Hill in the center with Pender and Anderson's divisions (Heth's in reserve); Longstreet on the left, leading the attack with Hood and McLaws. The attack was to sweep obliquely from left to right; Ewell was instructed to begin a strong diversion on the right when he heard Longstreet's guns.

A workable enough plan, but on 2 July it was bungled by everybody – though there was enough of a blunder on the Union side to give Lee's plan a good chance of working. To begin with, Ewell balked at attacking entrenched Union positions on Culp's and Cemetery Hills; he made only a few ineffectual efforts during the day, far less than the major diversion intended. In any case, Ewell never got his signal from the right during the morning. Longstreet, supposed to attack on the Confederate right at dawn, delayed through the morning and into the afternoon, saying he was waiting for Pickett's fresh division, which had not yet arrived. Thus Longstreet was reluctant, Ewell waffling and Jackson sorely missed indeed.

But Longstreet's delay finally gave the Federals enough rope to nearly hang themselves. The blunder was accomplished by Union General Daniel E Sickles, who repeated his mistake at Chancellorsville by moving out of position. Sickles felt the ground occupied by his III Corps on the left flank, along the southern part of Cemetery Ridge, was not high enough; besides, there were Rebels out there moving toward his left. Itching for a fight, Sickles moved the III Corps forward without orders to slightly higher ground on a line from the Peach Orchard through the Wheat Field to Devil's Den. Watching from the heights, Generals Hancock and Gibbon saw Sickles's salient forming and accurately prophesied the outcome. About four o'clock in the afternoon a furious Meade rode over and ordered Sickles to pull the line back. As they argued, an earsplitting cannonade erupted square on Sickles's left flank – 46 of Longstreet's guns. Meade curtly observed that it was too late to pull back now: the III Corps would have to fight it out as best they could. Meade then galloped back to forestall the inevitable disaster – as best he could.

While part of the II Corps was ordered by Meade into Sickles's original position on Cemetery Ridge, Confederate infantry under John B Hood and Lafayette McLaws struck Sickles's salient about five o'clock. The rest of the Union Army looked on helplessly as Hood's men, despite the wounding of Hood himself, routed the Union position in Devil's Den and swarmed around the left flank and up Round Top. By six, Sickles had been carried from the field minus a leg and General David B Birney had taken command, his left already giving way.

As Meade desperately shifted troops from his center and right toward the beleaguered left, the Rebels began moving north down Round Top toward Little Round Top. It was a disastrous prospect for the Army of the Potomac: if Little Round Top were to be taken, the Union left would crumble and Cemetery Ridge would no longer be defensible – Lee would roll up the Union Army like a rug, just as he had intended.

Now the fate of a great battle and of a nation concentrated on a small hill and on the actions of a very few men. One of these men, for a few critical moments the bearer of his nation's destiny, was General Gouverneur K Warren, Meade's chief engineer, who arrived at Little Round Top about this time. To his dismay, Warren saw that this place was the linchpin of the Union position and that there were no troops on it at all, only a signal station. He sent an imperative note to Meade and awaited results while watching Hood's forces – 500 men of the 15th Alabama – climbing toward him with shouts of victory.

As bullets began to fly around Warren, a few Federal cannon arrived and began sending canister into the enemy. Then at a run came 350 men of the 20th Maine commanded by young Colonel Joshua Chamberlain, who just one year before had left his position as Professor of Rhetoric at Bowdoin College to realize his dream of becoming a soldier. Now it was up to Chamberlain and the men of Maine to save or lose the Army of the Potomac.

Chamberlain's brigade commander, Colonel Strong Vincent, took him to the southern end of the hill, pointed to the advancing enemy and told Chamberlain to hold the ground at all costs. The 20th Maine spread out in a pitifully thin line, the sparse growth providing little cover. The charging Confederates crashed into the line and began pushing it back. The men of Maine fell in dozens, pulled back, but would not run: the exasperated Confederates could not dislodge them, even when their guns were in Federal faces. Then Chamberlain saw that his brigade's ammunition was nearly gone. What in God's name was left to do? Dazed and desperate, he ordered the only thing he could think of: 'Fix bayonets! Charge bayonets, charge!'

Their bayonets fixed, the men hesitated before this suicidal prospect. Suddenly Lieutenant H S Melcher ran out between the lines, into a hail of bullets, and shouted 'Come on! Come on, boys!' Here was another single man on whom the fulcrum of battle swung: the 20th Maine rose from their positions and with a scream of absolute anguish ran right into the Rebels.

The enemy had never seen anything like it (bayonet fighting was in fact rare in the war). In sheer shock, the Confederate line hesitated, then crumbled and ran back downhill. Their confusion was such that one Confederate officer was seen offering his sword in surrender with one hand while firing his pistol with the other. Heading for cover behind a stone wall below, the fleeing Southerners ran head-on into the rifles of the 20th Maine's skirmishers, who had been presumed killed.

Union General Daniel E Sickles.

For the moment the heroic men of the 20th Maine had saved the Federal left, but General Warren, still on the summit of Little Round Top, saw that the right of Strong Vincent's brigade was caving in. Trying to rally the men, Vincent himself was killed. Warren rode for help and grabbed the first troops he could find, the 140th New York, of Sykes's V Corps, which was now moving up from the rear. Coming up over Little Round Top at a dead run with unloaded guns and no bayonets, the New Yorkers simply charged straight at the enemy, their bodies their only weapons. Somehow this bizarre counterattack worked – the surprised Confederates pulled back. Little Round Top was safe, and Federal soldiers began piling in to reinforce it.

But no one could save the rest of the devastated III Corps. Surrounded by McLaws's men on three sides, Sickles's salient caved in, and McLaws made for the gap that opened up between the fleeing III Corps and Hancock's II Corps. From all over his line, Hancock, ordered by Meade to stop the rout, feverishly rushed troops to plug this gap. Again the battle came down to a few men, this time Union artillerymen around Trostle's Farm. There, just after seven o'clock, Artillery Captain John Bigelow held back William Barksdale's Mississippians long enough for a stronger battery to be mounted to the rear. Fighting surged into the artillery positions, the cannoneers beating back the Rebels with rammers, handspikes and fists; men rolled on the ground slug-

Opposite: Union soldiers in the field. *Below:* The Battle of Gettysburg, fought 1-3 July 1863 – a tragic clash of fellow countrymen on the eve of America's anniversary as a nation.

ging away like barroom rowdies. At last Barksdale was killed and his Mississippians could not get through the gap.

It had been a day of almosts for the Confederacy, but Lee was by no means finished yet. Southern efforts were shifting steadily northward; the next blow came in the Federal Center on Cemetery Ridge. Hancock, commanding that part of the field, saw a flag moving toward him, apparently from his own lines. He asked angrily why his men were re-treating: a volley showed him that it was a Rebel column, some 50 yards away. Hancock rode back and found Colonel Colville of the 1st Minnesota. 'Do you see those colours?,' Hancock demanded. Colville did. 'Well, capture them!' he shouted. Still in marching column, the 1st Minnesota charged the Confederates, who fell back and then rallied, get-ting the Federals into a pocket. The Minnesotans' line held on somehow, and when the Confederates finally fell back, the 1st Minnesota had 47 men left of the 262 who had charged so gallantly – 82 percent casualties, the worst of the war.

Confederate attacks on the left and center of the Federal line had failed, each seemingly by a hair's breadth. The Union staff had finally learned to maneuver their troops to best advantage on the battlefield, just as Lee had always done. And the Army of the Potomac had fought as well as anyone could have asked. As the fighting began to die down on the center and left, the Confederates settled into

position at the base of the Round Tops, in Devil's Den and along the base of Cemetery Ridge.

About six in the evening there had been a threat to the Federal right. After an artillery barrage Ewell finally made a move on Culp's Hill, held by Howard's XI Corps. Federal strength there was de-

pleted due to troops being sent south. Edward Johnson's brigade, on the Confederate right, advanced up the hill toward strong but sparsely manned Union breastworks. Again Federal reinforcements arrived in time to stop the attack, and after eight o'clock Johnson's men settled into position on the slopes.

An hour later, in the last fighting of 2 July, Jubal Early's Confederates made it into XI Corps batteries

A Rebel sharpshooter
succumbs to exhaustion
at Gettysburg.

on Cemetery Hill. For the second time that day, Union cannoneers and Rebel infantry fought hand-to-hand, the Union's so-called Dutchmen cursing vigorously in German. After an hour of bitter fighting, Early called it quits when Federal reinforcements arrived for a countercharge. Except for a few confused attempts on Culp's Hill by Ewell's men during the night, the second day's fighting was finally done.

The quiet Pennsylvania countryside echoes to the roar of guns under the pall of smoke at Gettysburg.

In battle, chaos and horror are the norm, and soldiers in the heat of fighting learn of necessity to shut it out, to concentrate on loading, on shooting, on dressing the lines. But when battle is done the horror of it all returns suddenly in the silence. A Union survivor wrote of that moment, 'There was no rebellion here now – the men of South Carolina were quiet by the side of those of Massachusetts, some composed with upturned faces, sleeping the last sleep, some mutilated and frightful, some wretched, fallen, bathed in blood, survivors still, and unwilling witnesses of the rage of Gettysburg.'

Still, for the Union survivors that night there was the strange and profound joy of armies after battle – the joy of having come alive to the other side of hell, and the comradeship amounting almost to love for those who shared that journey at one's side. The Union men knew they had fought well; Lee had thrown his whole army at them and they had held the line. In the Southern camps there was perhaps less celebration, but no real discouragement either. The Army of Northern Virginia was not used to defeat, and they by no means felt defeated now. They were certain that Lee would know what to do to finish off the Yankees tomorrow.

In the middle of the night General Meade took the unusual step of assembling his staff for a council of war. They met in the small shabby farmhouse that was his headquarters. The youngest man attending was General Howard, age 35; Meade, at 45, was the oldest. The Army of the Potomac had lost some 20,000 men in two days of fighting. Now Meade wanted a consensus on what to do next: should they retreat, attack, or wait for Lee to attack? The decision was quick and nearly unanimous: they would wait for the Confederate attack. As the generals left, Meade took aside John Gibbon, former commander of the Iron Brigade, who had three brothers in the Southern Army and was to command troops in every remaining major battle of the east. 'If Lee attacks tomorrow,' Meade told Gibbon, 'it will be in your front.'

Dawn broke and the Union Army looked out from the heights and waited. Over on the right, at Culp's Hill, there was soon some action – inconclusive, but another small tragedy in a sea of tragedies. Ewell opened up a cannonade and then sent his men up the hill. But the Federals, in good log-reinforced trenches, turned back the attack with impunity. Then an order from some Union commander went out to scout the Rebel lines a bit; for some reason this reached the 2nd Massachusetts and 27th Indiana as an order for a counterattack. Colonel Charles R Mudge, in command, shrugged 'It is murder, but that's the order.' He led his two regiments down into the enemy line and they were cut to pieces, losing a colonel, four color bearers and 250 men including Colonel Mudge. Following this pointless tragedy another Confederate charge was mounted and broke apart with heavy losses. Ewell finally realized that he had been right, that he could not take Culp's Hill. About 10:30 a deep silence spread once again over the battlefield.

The Confederacy's 'scorched-earth' policy demanded the destruction of everything in the path of advancing Union Armies, a major factor in the South's long-drawn-out recovery from the conflict.

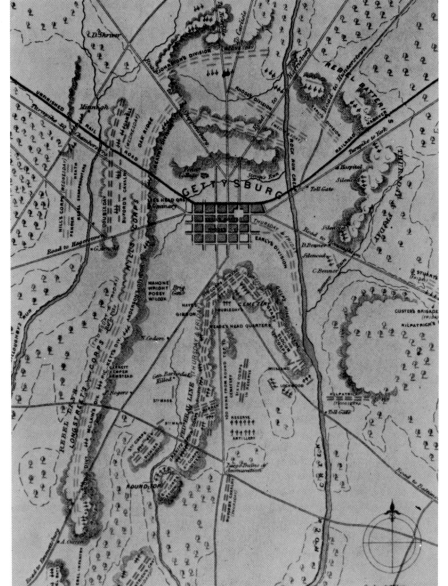

Left: The high cost of victory at Gettysburg, where over 7000 soldiers of both sides lost their lives.
Below: The scene of battle at Gettysburg.

Again the Union Army waited, resting on their arms. As the morning haze burned off, the day became clear and oppressively hot. Meade tinkered with his dispositions. His lines were still in the shape of a fishhook, Slocum behind in the east and curving to Culp's Hill, Howard from there over to Cemetery Hill, then Gibbon, Hancock (now commanding the III Corps after Sickles's injury), Sykes on the ridge to the Round Tops, Sedgwick and cavalry commander Judson Kilpatrick protecting the left flank.

But for some reason the middle was stinted this time, despite Meade's prediction of the night before. In the Union middle stood 6000 men of the Second and Third Divisions of the II Corps under Gibbon. The two divisions lay mostly along a stone fence so low the men had to lie or kneel behind it to gain cover. Near the middle of the fence was a little clump of trees, at which point the fence made a dogleg. Behind it were artillery and infantry positioned to fire over the heads of the men in front. It was perhaps the weakest part of the entire Union line.

As the fighting on the right died down, the waiting Federals began to see enemy activity on Seminary Ridge, across the way. Many cannon were being moved into position – a wall of cannon in clear view, their empty muzzles glinting in the late-morning sun as they pointed toward the Union Army. Finally there was a line nearly two miles long, some 150 guns. Opposing them on the Federal side were less than a hundred cannon.

The silence prevailed as noon approached: Hancock opined that the batteries were covering a Confederate retreat. Gibbon was not at all sure about that, but he was sure that he was getting hungry. He invited Meade, Hancock and some other officers to join him behind the II Corps lines to reconnoiter a bit of stewed chicken. There were even a few potatoes to be had, and a big loaf of bread only a little the worse for wear from an encounter with a hog. If the chickens, objectively speaking, were a little old, no one dreamed of complaining. During lunch Meade shifted Hancock back to his II Corps command and Gibbon to the Second Division. About 12:30 PM Meade excused himself; the others wandered off or lay lolling in the sun.

Now what was that sound dully striking the quiet afternoon air? On the front line the dozing Federals sat up and looked across: a puff of smoke was drifting up from one of the Rebel guns. It was one o'clock. Then, instant and unbelievable pandemonium. All 150 Rebel guns roared at once. The Federal position erupted in a hail of fire and iron. Men died while lighting cigars, with food halfway to their mouths; wagons, trees, horses, men and the very earth itself exploded into the air. As one veteran described the sound: 'Some of the shot shrieked and hissed, some whistled; some came with a muffled growl; some with howls like rushing, circling winds. Some spat and sputtered; others uttered unearthly groans. . . . Holes like graves were gouged in the earth by exploding shells. If a constellation of meteoric worlds had exploded above our heads, it would scarcely have been more terrible than this iron rain.' And under it all, nearly drowned but still horribly distinct, were the screams of maimed and dying men and animals.

The Union guns opened in reply, commanders cautioning their gunners to conserve ammunition. For now it was certain what was happening: this was only the prelude to a major assault that would fall where the cannonade was hottest – the II Corps, just as Meade had predicted. Despite the indescribable confusion of men, horses and wagons behind the Federal lines, it became clear that the Confederate gunners were making a fatal mistake – they were firing just a shade too high. As a result, the Union front line, where the coming attack would fall, was scarcely touched by the shells. Instead they fell behind the crest of the ridge on the Union rear, including Meade's headquarters. Meade and his staff huddled for a while behind the farmhouse as shells tore through the thin walls, Meade joking and the rest trying to laugh. Finally they moved back.

It went on for an hour and a half, the worst cannonade ever on American soil and perhaps on any soil to that time. Then slowly it slackened, fell away, died; by three o'clock in the afternoon there was ominous silence again. The men of the II Corps rose to their feet and looked out over the open fields of grain in their front for several minutes. Then they saw something that took their breaths away, something they would never forget: 15,000 of their enemy dressed immaculately on a front half a mile wide and three ranks deep, colors flying, sunlight flashing on musket barrels and drawn swords, officers galloping up and down, the men's steps firm

A hard-fought action.

and determined. Silently, the Union men watched their enemy approach. For the last time in the war, perhaps for the last time in history, it was to be a grand charge in the old Napoleonic style, and it was a terrible and magnificent thing to behold.

But once again, things were not as they appeared in the Army of Northern Virginia. That morning Longstreet had struggled for the last time to convince Lee of the necessity for a defensive strategy – a strategic envelopment on the Union right. In reply Lee had pointed imperiously with his fist to Cemetery Hill, saying 'The enemy is there, and I am going to strike him.' Greatly agitated, Longstreet argued 'General, I have been a soldier all my life. It is my opinion that no 15,000 men ever arrayed for battle can take that position.' Lee, calm as always, proceeded to give his orders.

Longstreet was an old soldier, so he carried out the orders whose outcome he knew only too well. That morning was his Gethsemane. The charge was to be under his command.

The artillery was positioned and the barrage executed, the Rebel guns exhausting most of their ammunition. While the guns were firing Longstreet arranged the lines. In front were two divisions, J Johnston Pettigrew on the left and the fresh troops of George E Pickett on the right. To the middle rear was the division of Isaac R Trimble (a mistake in placement, for Trimble was supposed to be in **echelon** to the left, supporting that flank where fire **would be heaviest**). Hill and Ewell had been ordered

to support the charge, but they did almost nothing.

For some reason history decided to call this action 'Pickett's Charge,' although Longstreet was actually in command. But General George Pickett was certainly one of the most enthusiastic soldiers on the field. A perfumed dandy, Pickett had been last in his class at West Point, and indeed would probably not have gotten in at all without the influence of his good friend Abraham Lincoln – whose name Pickett would not allow to be slandered in his presence. But Pickett made a dashing soldier, and he had a sweetheart, a girl of nineteen to whom he wrote daily. On this day Pickett wrote her twice, before and after the charge. Minutes before his division moved out, he described the scene that would remain engraved on his memory:

Our line of battle faces Cemetery Ridge. The men are lying in the rear, and the hot July sun pours its scorching rays almost vertically down on them. The suffering is almost unbearable. I have never seen Old Peter [Longstreet] so grave and troubled. For several minutes after I had saluted him he looked at me without speaking. Then in an agonized voice, the reserve all gone, he said, 'Pickett, I am being crucified. I have instructed Alexander to give you your orders, for I can't.'

While he was yet speaking, a note was brought to me from Alexander. After reading it I handed it to Pete, asking if I should obey and go forward. He looked at me for a moment, then held out his

'Pickett's Charge' at Gettysburg threw a shadow over the career of the controversial Confederate general who was, in fact, minimally responsible for the fatal action.

regiments, who open up a blistering musket fire.

A hundred yards away now. Soon the left side of the Federal line is firing; the Confederates on that flank begin drifting to their left, toward the angle at the little clump of trees. The 8th Ohio, posted forward as skirmishers, enfilades the Confederate left; the flank disappears in smoke. Both Rebel flanks begin to falter, then the left gives way. But the center moves forward still. Pettigrew is down, Generals Garnett and Kemper of Pickett's corps are mortally wounded.

Alonzo Cushing has one gun left; he orders it wheeled down to the stone wall to fire point-blank with triple-shotted canister into the oncoming mass of Rebels. He fires his last charge just as a fatal bullet finds him. The Rebel spearhead is at the wall now, and some have leaped over it. They are led by General Lewis Armistead, holding his hat on his sword to show his men the way. Armistead is headed for a strange rendezvous with one of his oldest and dearest friends, General Winfield Scott Hancock.

This is the high tide of the Confederacy. Armistead and a handful of men are over the wall; the Rebel colors are arriving one after another; the Rebels are among Cushing's wrecked battery. Armistead himself grasps one of the guns. Gibbon and Hancock are wounded, and Pennsylvanians are retreating from the overrun angle. In this small place and time, the issue is to be decided. All is

Above: Confederate prisoners after Gettysburg.
Right: Confederate General George E Pickett, whose letters from the field provided a combatant's account of the carnage at Gettysburg.

Opposite: Union General William S Rosecrans at the head of his troops.

hand. . . . I shall never forget the look in his face nor the clasp of his hand, and I saw tears glistening on his cheeks and beard. The stern old war horse, God bless him, was weeping for his men and, I know, praying too that this cup might pass from them. It is almost three o'clock.

YOUR SOLDIER

On Cemetery Ridge the men of the II Corps watched in awe for a while. Then they got down to business – guns loaded and cocked, thumbs checking the percussion caps, cartridges lined up to hand on the ground. With a running rattle, thousands of muskets stretched out over the stone wall. Lieutenant Alonzo Cushing of Battery 4A, wounded three times in the Rebel cannonade, was being propped by a sergeant amid the wreckage of his battery; his two remaining guns awaited his orders. The Confederate lines marched across half a mile of open fields, the grain parting gently before them; they moved over the plank fences of the Emmitsburg Road, closing in toward the little clump of trees at the angle of the stone wall on Cemetery Ridge. The Federal artillery watched, poised: There, in range! 'Fire!'

Now a storm of shell opens into the Rebels. Holes appear in their lines, colors fall and are retrieved. Still the men march steadily forward. Now they come into shrapnel range, now into canister range. Southerners fall in tens, in hundreds; great gaps are torn in the lines. Across the way the Rebel batteries have few shells to fire in reply. The Confederate right flank brushes past some concealed Vermont

smoke and fire and indecipherable chaos on the open brow of the ridge. Struggling hand to hand in mortal combat, the men of both armies are not cheering or shouting, but growling like animals, making a sound strange and terrible, like a vast mournful roar.'

Things happen fast now. The Pennsylvanians rally and surge forward. Reinforcements come from somewhere. A leaderless horde of Federals swarms around the enemy spearhead, while Union cannons continue tearing apart the Rebels in front. Armistead is down, gasping out his life.

All at once, it is finished. The Confederate spearhead seems to dissolve. Some Southerners fall back; others throw down their muskets, raising their hands in surrender. The Confederacy has reached its high-water mark, has receded, and the crest of Cemetery Ridge is won. The irresistible charge of a few minutes before becomes a rabble of survivors pouring back down the slope to their own lines and safety.

Meade rides up from the rear, his face very white, and inquires of Lieutenant Franklin Haskell 'How is it going here?' 'I believe, General, the enemy is repulsed,' Haskell replies. 'Thank God,' Meade says, and adds a choked cheer.

Lying on a stretcher dictating orders, Hancock is interrupted by an aide, who hands him a watch and a few personal effects. They are from Armistead, whose last words were a message to his old friend: 'Tell Hancock I have done him and my country a

Below left: Lincoln giving his Gettysburg Address, to a crowd of 15,000. The President believed his words at Gettysburg were destined for oblivion (a contemporary newspaper reported only that 'The President also spoke'). Contrary to popular belief, Lincoln had not composed his address in haste but had labored over every line with deep emotion.
Below right: Union prisoners at Richmond's Libby Prison.

great injustice which I shall never cease to regret.' But all regrets are over for Armistead.

Strewn with thousands of dead and wounded, the battleground looked, as one soldier remarked, like 'a square mile of Tophet.' Across the way the beaten Confederates sank exhausted into their lines, to be visited by Lee who said, and meant it, 'All this has been my fault.' Even Stuart, finally arrived the previous night, had been repulsed today by Federal cavalry on the north flank. For the Army of Northern Virginia it was complete and unmitigated defeat that third of July. A prostrated Pickett wrote again to his sweetheart: 'My brave boys were so full of hope and confident of victory as I led them forth! Well, it's all over now. The awful rain of shot and shell. . . Oh, how faithfully they followed me on – on – to their death, and I led them on . . . Oh, God!'

But there was still work to be done. The Confederates next day formed their lines and waited for the counterattack that never came – the Army of the Potomac was too hurt and exhausted for that. In the afternoon of 4 July a downpour began, washing the blood from the grass. Maintaining his lines, Lee buried his dead and evacuated his wounded on a long dismal wagon train that headed back to Virginia. The casualties were the worst of the war: of 88,289 Federals engaged, 3155 were killed, 14,529 wounded – many mortally – and 5365 missing, a total of 23,049 casualties. For the South, of 75,000 engaged, 3903 were killed, 18,735 wounded, 5425

missing, a total of 28,063. Lee had lost over a third of his army.

Reaching the Potomac, the Confederates found the waters swollen and halted on the banks to wait. Meade and his army pursued cautiously, paused before the entrenched enemy but did not attack. Lee's army withdrew across the receding Potomac the night of 13-14 July. Next day there was a rear-guard skirmish at Falling Waters, in which Heth lost 500 captured and Pettigrew was killed.

The high tide of the Confederacy had receded in the Eastern Theater. In Mississippi, on that very third of July, Vicksburg had fallen. Only a miracle could save the Confederacy now, and the South was running low on miracles.

Robert E Lee was a man unaccustomed to losing. In his youth he had been called the handsomest man in the US Army, and the best cadet in his class at West Point. He had gained honor, wealth and fame. But he had led a rebellion against his country, and now, in spite of many victories, he had helped to lose that rebellion. At Gettysburg he had made the mistake of Napoleon at Wagram and of Burnside at Fredericksburg – throwing a frontal attack against impregnable positions. He had overestimated his army and underestimated his enemy, who had re-quired only a modicum of good leadership to fight as well as they could, which turned out to be very well indeed. Now Lee had no choice but to do what Longstreet had begged him to do at the outset – go

on the defensive. But first he submitted his resig-nation to President Davis, assuming full responsi-bility for the defeat. Although he had not been served well by his generals at Gettysburg, he would not shift the blame. Davis refused the resignation, knowing that if the South had any hopes at all now, they were in Lee's hands. And Lee would prove to be a genius of defense as he had been a genius of offense.

Lee had escaped with his army, and thus there was to be more killing, no one knew for how long. Hearing the news of Lee's escape, an anguished Lincoln asked Secretary Welles, 'What does it mean? Great God! What does it mean?' A few months later, in his unforgettable words of dedica-tion for the dead at Gettysburg, Lincoln would begin to try and find that meaning.

Following pages: Gardner's photo The Field Where General Reynolds Fell.

Below: Harvest of Death, July 1863, from Gardner's Photographic Sketch Book of the War.

CHAPTER EIGHT

CHICKAMAUGA
BATTLE ON THE RIVER OF DEATH

THE YEAR 1863 WAS decisive for the conflict: the fortunes of war turned the corner that would lead inexorably to Union victory. Ironically, that year of decisive struggle was ushered in by the indecisive battle of Stones River, near Murfreesboro, Tennessee. There, in three days of fighting between the Federal Army of the Cumberland and the Confederate Army of Tennessee, 20,000 men fell to no advantage to either side. For nearly six months thereafter these two armies sat some 40 miles apart, waiting for their next confrontation.

Commanding the Southern forces was General Braxton Bragg, a trusted friend of President Jefferson Davis. That friendship was not to bode well for the Confederacy. Bragg was an intelligent man but a poor leader, a great maker of plans who could not bring them to fruition. Harsh, argumentative and inflexible, he was not liked by his subordinates and was served badly by them (no doubt partly because they knew he would be quick to make them scapegoats for his own mistakes).

His Union counterpart, General William S Rosecrans, had earned his command by demonstrating a talent for strategy. Early in the war Rosecrans had driven the Confederates from West Virginia, and later had been of great service to Grant in Mississippi. His men affectionately called him 'Old Rosey,' and were nearly as fond of him as the Army of the Potomac had been of McClellan. Like McClellan, Rosecrans was meticulous in planning

campaigns down to the last wagonwheel; also like McClellan, he was maddeningly slow to move. After the standoff in Murfreesboro, the obvious goal of his army was the last truly vital city of the Confederacy: Chattanooga.

The city lies in the southeastern corner of Tennessee near the borders of Alabama and Georgia, on the banks of the Tennessee River. Railroads converged on it from all over the South, making Chattanooga the strategic center of the Confederacy. If it were to be conquered by the Union, much of the Southern war effort would be slowed literally to a walk. In giving Rosecrans that task, Washington gave him an immense responsibility.

In the first six months of 1863 the Confederate Army of Tennessee lay in Tullahoma, on the road between Rosecrans's army (near Murfreesboro) and Chattanooga. In May Washington began to pressure Rosecrans to move against Bragg; this would not only threaten Chattanooga, but keep Bragg from sending men to reinforce Vicksburg, which was now besieged by Grant. Rosecrans waffled and Bragg did send some troops to Mississippi.

In mid-June Rosecrans finally got his army moving and at once demonstrated his strategic skills. He threatened the Rebel left flank with cavalry, and when Bragg attempted to meet this threat he discovered that two Union corps, those of George H Thomas and Thomas L Crittenden, had gotten behind the Confederate right. Confused and helpless, Bragg was forced after 30 June to pull back to his nearest stronghold – Chattanooga.

It had been a brilliant tactical move, but then Rosecrans sat down again, asking for reinforcements – which were soon available, for Vicksburg fell in early July. But the Federal General-in-Chief Henry Halleck, obsessed with occupying conquered territory, spread Grant's forces all over the western Confederacy and would send none to Rosecrans. Meanwhile, Bragg was heavily reinforced, most notably in mid-July by General David H Hill, formerly with Lee's army; also on the way were two divisions under General James Longstreet, which were now available after the Confederate defeat at Gettysburg. (Longstreet had suggested a move much like this well before Gettysburg, which might have saved both Vicksburg and Chattanooga.)

On 5 August Halleck ordered Rosecrans to move on Bragg, and also sent forces from Kentucky under Ambrose Burnside to occupy Knoxville. Now Rosecrans faced the problem of getting Bragg out of heavily fortified Chattanooga. He tried another strategic dodge and it appeared to work handsomely, abetted by Bragg's almost nonexistent intelligence-gathering: Federal columns appeared along the Tennessee River at several widely spaced points; as Bragg hesitated, worrying about his supply line to the rear, the Federal Army crossed the river unopposed west of the city and Crittenden marched on Chattanooga.

Rosecrans soon learned that Bragg was pulling out of the city (6 September) and moving south into

Georgia. This was actually a wise move on Bragg's part: he was doing what Pemberton had failed to do at Vicksburg – get out of town with his army while the getting was good. Certain, however, that their enemy was fleeing, the Federals made haste to pursue them into Georgia. Crittenden marched through Chattanooga and then turned south across the ridges. Through two other widely spaced mountain passes moved the corps of Thomas and Alexander McCook. The Federals were beginning to talk about chasing Bragg to Atlanta, if not clear to the sea.

But in fact Rosecrans was making two big mistakes. He had claimed his goal, Chattanooga, and should have been satisfied with it for the moment. And worse, Bragg was by no means fleeing. Instead, the Confederates were concentrating near Lafayette, Georgia, and preparing to turn and destroy the Federal Army. Rosecrans and his men were thus marching recklessly into a trap. Whether Bragg had actually planned the trap is uncertain – D H Hill later insisted his commander was as confused as ever – but it is still true that the Confederates had their enemy in a very tight spot indeed. Or rather, a very loose spot: the three Union corps were spread out over 50 miles of rugged country, moving through three narrow gaps in the long ridge called Lookout Mountain. Crittenden was in the north, Thomas in the middle and McCook far to the south. Bragg had merely to bring his superior numbers to bear and crush them in detail, one corps at a time. The Federal Army was ripe for the picking.

Deliberate trap or not, Bragg and his generals proceeded to spring it ineptly. The forces of General Leonidas Polk were ordered to attack Thomas on 10 September. Though Polk's men appeared in Thomas's path, nothing happened. Another attack failed to be mounted on the 11th. On the 13th Bragg arrived at Lee and Gordon's Mill, on Chickamauga Creek, expecting Polk to have annihilated Crittenden's corps there. Polk had not budged. D H Hill would later compare Bragg's methods to Jackson's, which Hill had observed first hand: 'Whenever a great battle is to be fought, the commander must be on the field to see that his orders are executed and to take advantage of the ever-changing phases of the conflict. Jackson leading a cavalry fight by night near Front Royal . . ., Jackson at the head of the column following McClellan, presents a contrast to Bragg sending from a distance of ten miles, four consecutive orders [to Polk] for an attack at daylight, which he was never to witness.'

The fact that his corps kept finding parties of Confederates in their front, all of whom seemed to be withdrawing toward Lafayette, finally tipped off Rosecrans that he was in serious trouble. On 12 September he urgently ordered his wings to move toward the center and to concentrate on the west side of Chickamauga Creek, near Lafayette. McCook's men began a heroic 57-mile journey north through the mountains that brought them to the rest of the Federal Army on 17 September. Bragg

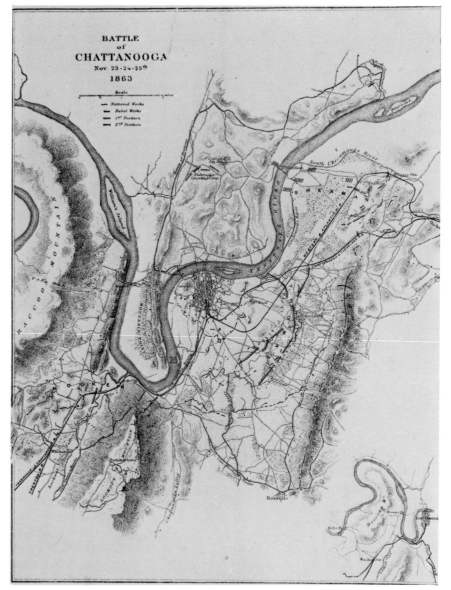

meanwhile was concentrating his forces near the creek and impatiently awaiting Longstreet's divisions. When they arrived Bragg would have over 65,000 men to Rosecrans's less than 60,000.

Rosecrans had divined (apparently before Bragg himself did) that the Confederates' best tactic would be to move around the Federal left and cut off their line of retreat – a road through Rossville, Georgia, to Chattanooga. He paid special attention to his left, then, placing George H Thomas in command there. Whether or not this was fortuitous, the positioning of the indomitable Thomas was a fortunate decision for the Union Army. (Years before, Thomas had been a lieutenant in Bragg's artillery battery – the two other lieutenants in that battery being D H Hill and John Reynolds, the latter killed at Gettysburg. Bragg still spoke fondly of Thomas.)

Commanding the middle of Rosecrans's line was Thomas L Crittenden, whose father was a notable Senator and brother a Confederate general. On the right was Alexander McCook, one of a large tribe called the 'fighting McCooks of Ohio.' Two of his brothers and a cousin were fellow officers in the Army of the Cumberland. But Rosecrans's deploy-

Site view of the Battle of Chattanooga, 23-25 November 1863.

Opposite left: The Battle of Lookout Mountain, 24 November 1863.
Right: Lookout Mountain, where overconfident General Braxton Bragg assured an anxious bystander that 'There are not enough Yankees in Chattanooga to come up here.'
Below: The Battle of Stones River, near Murfreesboro, Tennessee.

ment was not well in position until 19 September. Bragg, having lost his golden opportunity to destroy the Federals in the passes, issued orders for an attack on the Federal left (north) flank at dawn on the 18th. This attack could have overwhelmed the Federals at that point, but it was frustrated by Union cavalry and never developed. Now Bragg and his subordinates had co-operated to lose a pretty collection of opportunities. But they still had some left.

The night of the 18th, both sides prepared for battle, Rosecrans building a strong defensive position. Because of the thick woods in the area, neither general knew quite where his enemy was – or, indeed, where his own forces were. Bragg thought the Union left was at Lee and Gordon's Mill, and planned his attack to flank that position and gain the road to Chattanooga. Since Rosecrans had anticipated this, he had strung his lines out north from the mill and along the road. By daybreak on the 19th Thomas's men had reached Kelly Farm and formed line of battle around a steep horseshoe ridge in front of the Kelly house.

As day came on the 19th, both armies were poised for battle at Chickamauga Creek. Prophetically, the creek's name came from an old Cherokee word meaning 'River of Death.' A Union captain remem-

bered the feelings of his men that morning: 'Through that forenoon we saw the constantly moving columns of the enemy's infantry and saw battery after battery as they moved before us like a great panorama. In such moments men grow pale and lose their nerve. They are hungry, but they can not eat; they are tired, but they can not sit down. You speak to them, and they answer as if half asleep; they laugh, but the laugh has no joy in it.'

It began by accident. Unsure whether there were Confederates north of the creek, Thomas sent cavalry to scout his front. Soon the Federals stumbled on some of Nathan Bedford Forrest's cavalrymen who were dismounted on the Reed's Bridge road. The Rebels retreated under fire back to their infantry, who then pushed forward. Slowly the battle spread outward until both armies were firing all along the line.

There followed a confused but destructive day of fighting. As Hill later wrote, 'It was the sparring of the amateur boxer, not the crushing blows of the trained pugilist.' All morning there was a gap of some two miles in the Federal lines between Crittenden and Thomas, but Bragg failed to find or to exploit it. Most of the Confederate efforts were thrown where Rosecrans expected, at Thomas's lines on the left. Rosecrans sat in his headquarters with field telegraphs (an innovation of the era) clicking away; one line came directly from Thomas, who continually asked for reinforcements, and got them. Thus the Union lines steadily extended to the north. At one point the Confederates (led by John B Hood, whose division had arrived ahead of his commander Longstreet's other forces) smashed the right center of the Union line and got onto the

Union forces survey the scene of battle at Chattanooga.

Above: The fighting near Orchard Knob, 24 November 1863.
Below: James A Garfield was one of several Union generals who went on to become President of the United States.

Chattanooga road, but a wave of Federals charged in to drive them back. On the Union left the courageous Thomas maintained the advantage.

After a day of heavy but indecisive fighting the guns fell silent in the late afternoon. Win, lose, or draw, the outcome for the unlucky was the same – dead men blanketed the thick woods, the wounded staggered, crawled, or were carried to the rear, surgeons labored in the field hospitals.

In mid-afternoon Longstreet had arrived by rail with the rest of his forces. It took him until 11:00 PM to find General Bragg, who got out of bed for a conference. Dividing his army into two wings, Bragg gave the right to Polk, commanding the corps of Hill and Walker, the division of Cheatham, and Forrest's cavalry. Commanding the left wing was Longstreet, with the divisions of Hood, Hindman and Buckner and cavalry under Wheeler. Polk was to begin with a strong assault at dawn on Thomas – again, the Union left was the primary target. After Polk's offensive, there were to be successive attacks down the line to the south.

As the Confederate generals spoke they heard the sound of axes from the Federal lines – the Army of the Cumberland was building a strong defensive line of log breastworks. Meanwhile, at the Federal

council of war, Rosecrans heard reports and suggestions while an exhausted Thomas dozed in his chair. Each time he was addressed, Thomas would awake and proclaim 'Strengthen the left!', and each time Rosecrans would respond, 'Where are we going to take the men from?' Thomas was finally ordered to hold his position on the horseshoe ridge at all costs, and Crittenden and McCook were cautioned to keep closed up toward the left. This latter element of the day's instructions was the beginning of a complex chain of circumstances of great import on the following day.

At dawn on 20 September visibility was negligible due to the woods and a thick blanket of fog. Bragg sat in his headquarters straining to hear the sound of Polk's attack. After an hour of inactivity, a messenger was dispatched to find Polk. The general – who was also an Episcopal bishop – was discovered breakfasting comfortably in a farmhouse. Queried about his attack, Bishop Polk responded grandly 'Do tell General Bragg that my heart is overflowing with anxiety for the attack – overflowing with anxiety, sir!' When this was reported to Bragg, he cursed 'in a manner that would have powerfully assisted a mule team in getting up a mountain' and ordered the attack on Thomas begun immediately.

By this time the front stretched some two miles north to south. The Confederates fell with a will upon Thomas, who held onto his breastworks in the horseshoe-ridge salient but soon found his flank being pushed across the vital road to Chattanooga. Again and again Thomas called for reinforcements from Rosecrans. Confusion began to creep into Union deployments: before the attack Rosecrans had ordered James S Negley's reserve to reinforce Thomas. However, it was discovered that Negley was in line instead of in reserve, and Thomas J Wood's division in reserve where Negley's was supposed to be. Some of Negley's men were pulled out and sent to Thomas, while Wood moved up into line. But the confusion continued. Negley and his men got lost, wandering back to Rossville; Rosecrans meanwhile assumed that Negley was in position with Thomas. Then, after two hours of fighting, his left flank in peril, Thomas again sent an imperative call for reinforcements.

At 11:00 AM the mounting Federal confusion helped create a strange and catastrophic turn in the battle. As Rosecrans was trying desperately to find men to send to Thomas, an aide, who had been riding behind the Union position, reported that there was a gap in the Federal line between Wood's and J J Reynold's division. Intending to seal that gap, Rosecrans hurriedly sent an order to General Wood to move left, to 'close up on and support' Reynolds. (Both these corps lay near the Federal right flank, which was so far inactive.)

But the aide had made a disastrous mistake: there was no gap in the Union line. Between Wood and Reynolds was John Brannan's division, exactly where they were supposed to be, but so hidden by the thick woods that the aide had not seen them. Thus the actual positions were Reynolds-Brannan-Wood.

Wood received Rosecrans's order and puzzled over it. How could he close up on and support Reynolds when there was another division between them? Finally, he decided that 'support' was the

New York Herald correspondents in the field, 1863. The Civil War was the first to be widely and consistently covered by the popular press.

The war reached as far south as Florida where the Battle of Olustee was fought – 20 February 1864.

Below: Civil War artist Alfred R Waud, a correspondent for *Harper's Weekly*, shown sketching in the field in a famous photograph by Matthew Brady.

operative idea and ordered his division to pull out of line and march behind Brannan toward Reynolds. His men formed line of march and headed for the rear, leaving a gaping hole in the Union right wing.

At that moment, hardly a stone's throw away but still hidden in the woods, Longstreet was massing eight brigades for attack. (That the attack was gathering then and there was apparently sheer coincidence.) At the head of the column rode hard-fighting John B Hood. Around 11:30 the Rebels headed for the Union lines and found to their astonishment that no one was there. The results were immediate and dramatic. A solid column of screaming Rebels flooded straight through the Union line, crashed onto the end of Wood's departing column and scattered the divisions of Federal Generals Philip Sheridan and Jefferson C Davis, who had begun moving into the gap from the right. Hood, having lost the use of an arm at Gettysburg, was now wounded seriously in the leg, but his men pushed on.

At Rosecrans's headquarters an observer described that moment:

I had not slept much for two nights and lay down on the grass. I was awakened by the most infernal noise I ever heard. I sat up, and the first thing I saw was General Rosecrans crossing himself – he was a very devout Catholic. 'Hello!' I said to myself. 'if the general is crossing himself, we are in a desperate situation.' I looked around toward the front where all this din came from, and I saw our lines break and melt away like leaves before the wind. Then the headquarters around me disappeared. The graybacks came through with a rush, and soon the musket balls and the cannon shot began to reach the place where we stood. The whole right of the army had apparently been routed.

Wheeling his forces to the north, Longstreet sent the right wing of the Federal Army scurrying up the road toward Chattanooga. During this rout the Federals lost thousands in casualties and captured; Hill later wrote that he had not seen so many Federal dead since the suicidal charge at Fredericksburg. Among those fleeing were McCook, Crittenden and

a panicky and demoralized Rosecrans. In Rossville Rosecrans discovered Negley, who was supposed to be with Thomas. The sight of Negley clinched it: assuming that his whole army was routed, Rosecrans ordered everyone to retreat to Chattanooga (an order fortunately not obeyed by all). Rosecrans was wrong. Along the horseshoe ridge to the left, called Snodgrass Hill, Thomas, with the whole Rebel army swarming around him, was holding on like grim death. Meanwhile, at Confederate headquarters Longstreet was begging General Bragg to give him reinforcements to surround Snodgrass Hill. Bragg, apparently of the opinion that his army was losing, replied that the rest of the men had 'no fight left in them.' Bragg had withheld no reinforcements and clearly had little idea of the fighting abilities of Longstreet and his men.

By mid-afternoon Thomas was watching Longstreet's forces move toward his right. He knew his front was strong – the slopes of the ridge were precipitous – but his flanks were in great danger. Fortunately, not all the routed Federal divisions had continued on to Chattanooga; Wood, Brannan and Reynolds fell into position on Thomas's right, Wood meeting Longstreet's first appearance with a determined bayonet charge that stopped the Rebels in their tracks.

As Thomas's line on the right stabilized a little, Rebel assaults swarmed onto the left flank. A Union participant remembered that 'In front stood the whole army of the enemy, eager to fall on us with the energy that comes from great success and greater hopes. But close behind our lines rode a general [Thomas] whose judgment never erred, whose calm, invincible will never bent; and around him thirty thousand soldiers resolved to exhaust the last round of ammunition, and then to hold their ground with their bayonets.'

It soon seemed that this extremity had been reached. The Federals were running out of ammunition, their front and flanks were staggering under heavy assaults, the enemy was moving around the right flank to the rear. Rebel cannon were moving into position to enfilade the Union right, and there were no men left to do anything about it. At 3:30 PM Thomas noticed a column of dust approaching in his rear: if this was the enemy, his men were doomed. An officer was dispatched to take a look.

The officer approached the oncoming column and called out 'Whose troops are these?'

'Mine, sir,' their general replied cautiously.

'General, may I inquire your name?'

'I am General Steedman, commanding the First Division of the Union Reserve Corps.'

Friends, then! It was one of two divisions of reserves commanded by General Gordon Granger, who had just committed a serious – and salutary – breach of orders. During the retreat of the right wing Granger's corps had been placed by Rosecrans to guard the road to Chattanooga, and enjoined to stay there at all costs. Since then Granger had listened with increasing anxiety to the sound of battle grow-

ing steadily on the Federal left. Finally, he made his own decision – 'I am going to Thomas, orders or no orders.' By four o'clock Granger was shaking hands

Top, center and *bottom:* Three of Alfred R Waud's vivid Civil War battle scenes.

with an overjoyed Thomas. Men and ammunition were arriving rapidly.

Showing Granger a gorge and ridge to the Union right and rear, which was full of Rebels, Thomas asked if Granger's men could drive them back. 'Yes,' Granger replied; 'My men are fresh, and they are just the fellows for that work. They are raw troops, and they don't know any better than to charge up there.'

Led by Steedman, the green Federals cheered and advanced into the valley, up the ridge into a murderous artillery and musket fire; they sent the enemy flying down the other side. Two more assaults on that ridge were mounted by the Confederates, but they too were sent back down the slopes.

Orders came from Rosecrans to retreat, but Thomas was determined to hold out until dark.

Ammunition was running low again; about six o'clock another Rebel charge on the left was turned back with bayonets. But at last dark came and Thomas withdrew his troops to Chattanooga. Behind him the exhausted Confederates finally placed their banner on the summit.

The South had won the field, but General George

Sutter's Row, Chattanooga, Tennessee.

Above: Confederate General Simon Bolivar Buckner.
Below: The fight for Missionary Ridge, which secured Chattanooga, strategic center of the Confederacy, for the Union.
Opposite page: Confederate General James Longstreet, who fought throughout the war.

Thomas had saved the Federal Army, becoming in the process one of the immortal heroes of the Union cause. He would be known to history as the 'Rock of Chickamauga.'

Casualties in the battle were among the worst of the war: of 58,222 Federals engaged, 1657 were killed, 9756 wounded, 4757 missing – a total of 16,170; for the South, of 66,326 engaged, there were 2312 killed, 14,674 wounded, 1468 missing for a total of 18,454. Altogether, nearly 35,000 men fell; both sides had lost 28 percent of their forces. For the South Chickamauga was a Pyrrhic victory, despite its tactical significance.

Back in his headquarters, Bragg could not seem to get it into his head that he had won. His generals pressed him to pursue, the impetuous Forrest proclaiming 'Every hour is worth a thousand men.' By next morning, 21 September, Bragg was finally willing to admit victory. He sent a force to Missionary Ridge in Chattanooga with orders to attack, but Bragg's men found the Federals 'ready to receive and entertain us.' The Union army had collected itself and entrenched; Bragg's pursuit was too late. But he had one more chance, and a perfectly good one at that, to reclaim Chattanooga. The Federals were now virtually besieged deep in enemy territory, Burnside powerless or unwilling to come to their relief from Knoxville. Bragg put his army in strong positions on the ridges around Chattanooga and

settled in to starve the Yankees out. And starve they did, while both Bragg and Rosecrans spent their time writing elaborate reports blaming their subordinates for everything.

It looked hopeless for the Union. Something had to be tried, but Rosecrans was clearly not the man to do it. Washington turned to the one leader it had who might be able to get the army out: on 23 October General Ulysses S Grant arrived in Chattanooga. He had been appointed to command of all Union forces west of the Alleghenies (except for Banks's in Mississippi). His first act was to replace Rosecrans with Thomas as Commander of the Army of the Cumberland.

Reinforced by his friend William T Sherman and by Joe Hooker, Grant soon had food and supplies flowing into Chattanooga. On 25 December the vindictive Federals, shouting 'Chickamauga!' as they charged, swarmed up the slopes of Missionary Ridge and chased the Confederate Army of Tennessee back to Georgia. Chattanooga, the strategic center of the Confederacy, was secure for the Union.

Now the nation turned to U S Grant as the man to beat Robert E Lee. At long last the North had a general who could win methodically and decisively and end the tragedy at last. In January 1864 Grant was summoned to Washington, to be given a great and terrible responsibility.

The Battle of
Spotsylvania, climax of
the Wilderness
Campaign.

CHAPTER NINE
SPOTSYLVANIA
GRANT HAMMERS AWAY

IN MARCH 1864 THE Federal Army of the Potomac got a look at the new General-in-Chief, Ulysses S Grant. It seemed they were going to be seeing a lot of him, for even though General George G Meade was still their nominal commander, with Grant responsible for the entire Union war effort, Grant had announced that his headquarters would be in the field with Meade.

The soldiers devoured newspapers, finding out what they could about Washington's chosen man. To them he looked pretty seedy for a commanding general, and not very commanding either. His expression was neither mild nor pugnacious – 'vacant' might describe it much of the time, though there was an unmistakable element of cold bulldog tenacity. Did he drink as much as rumor had it? How would this odd dual command work out? (Meade, after all, was not an accommodating type.) Most importantly, how would Grant match up to Bobby Lee? He had swallowed two whole armies in the South, but he was not fighting the likes of Pemberton and Bragg now; this was the East, the Big Top. The army was eager to see the outcome of Grant's clash with Lee.

An awesome responsibility had fallen on Grant's sagging shoulders. No one ever heard from him what that felt like. Instead of worrying aloud, he issued orders. There was to be a mammoth strategic offensive to end the war – the first time the North had had such a plan. There were to be simultaneous advances on five fronts: W T Sherman, now in Grant's old job commanding the Division of the Mississippi, was to march toward Atlanta; Ben Butler would move his army up the Peninsula toward the Confederate capital of Richmond; Franz Sigel would clear the Shenandoah Valley, cutting off the South's breadbasket; Nathaniel Banks would march on Mobile; Grant and Meade would move on Richmond from the north. It was a bold and seemingly irresistible strategy; however, in the next weeks Sigel, Banks and Butler were quick to fumble their part of it.

The prison camp at Andersonville, Georgia, where thousands of Union prisoners died of disease and malnutrition in 1864-65 as a result of deplorable conditions.

On 4 May 1864 the Army of the Potomac pulled out of Culpeper, Virginia, and headed again for Richmond, Grant intending to slip around Lee's right flank. The troops were considerably more cynical about their prospects than during McClellan's abortive 'On to Richmond' campaign of 1862. The two capitals were less than a hundred miles apart, but a seemingly uncrossable gulf yawned between them.

The Federal Army was stronger than ever, with 122,000 men newly organized into three corps under Winfield S Hancock (II), Gouverneur K Warren (V) and John Sedgwick (VI); supporting them, back on his old field of action in the East, was the genial and bumbling Ambrose E Burnside, commanding the IX Corps.

The army crossed the Rapidan and headed southeast on the most direct road to Richmond. They knew somewhere on that road Lee would be waiting for them. In two columns they marched nervously into the Wilderness, scene of their humiliation the year before in the battle of Chancellorsville. As Hooker had tried to do, Grant wanted to get his forces out of that jungle and into the open. As the men marched they saw the charred skeletons of their former mates in the gloomy woods. Then Grant got his first lesson about Robert E Lee: the Southern commander did not cotton to letting his enemy choose the time and place to fight. With his ragged and starving forces – just over half the strength of the Federals – Lee pounced on Grant's columns in the Wilderness. In the two days of fierce and confused fighting that ensued on 5-6 May, there was a near-repeat of Chancellorsville. The Federals were outfought and outgeneraled; again, hundreds burned to death in forest fires, and by the end of the second day James Longstreet's Confederates were rolling up the Federal lines. As disaster loomed for the Union, fate stepped in – Longstreet was seriously wounded by his own men (not five miles from where Stonewall Jackson had met the same fate a year before). With Longstreet down the Southern attack faltered, and both armies sank to a standstill. Losses were already staggering for the Union – 17,666 casualties, worse than at Antietam; Southern losses were uncounted, but probably less than half that figure.

It had been Longstreet who had warned his peers about Grant: 'That man will fight us every day and every hour till the end of the war.' Longstreet proved accurate; after the battle in the Wilderness the Rebels expected their enemy to retreat as usual. But Lee also knew his man, and knew better. To General John B Gordon, Lee observed, 'General Grant is not going to retreat. He will move his army to Spotsylvania. I am so sure of his next move that I have already made arrangements . . . to meet him there.' Lee was right. On the night of 7 May Grant shifted his forces around Lee's right flank and moved toward Spotsylvania – like Chancellorsville, another insignificant road crossing on the way to Richmond which was destined to have its name inscribed in blood. That day the Army of the Potomac began their march angrily, supposing they were 'on another skedaddle.' Suddenly they realized they were going south, not north – not retreating. During the march Grant appeared, slouched on his horse, moving to the head of the column. The exhausted men broke out in wild cheers and tossed their hats in the air. At last they had a general who would let them fight!

However, the Federals were going to have to fight before they expected to: Lee's forces were moving parallel to them in a desperate race to the crossroads. At dawn on 8 May the van of Warren's Corps reached the road between Todd's Tavern and Spotsylvania; to their astonishment the Federals found the enemy waiting for them. It was cavalry under Fitzhugh ('Fitz') Lee, Robert's nephew. The South had won the race. Almost too tired to walk, Warren's men formed line of battle as best they could. Fitz Lee was soon reinforced by Richard H Anderson, who now commanded Longstreet's forces. The Federals tried several feeble assaults, both of which were repulsed. At dusk, reinforced by Sedgwick, Warren tried one more attack in force. It too was futile. There would have to be another all-out battle, then – the second one that week.

During that day there had been an interesting scene at Union headquarters. When he came from Tennessee, Grant had brought with him to head his cavalry a short, feisty young general named Philip Sheridan. He was to become a legend of the war, but at this point Sheridan was new and an upstart. He had the notion that cavalry should be a real fighting arm rather than mere scouts and escorts.

That afternoon these issues came to a head in a violent quarrel. Meade greeted Sheridan with an angry accusation that in the race to Spotsylvania the cavalry had fatally impeded Warren's infantry – which was true. Sheridan retorted that it had happened because Meade had countermanded his orders – also true. After a lively shouting match

Sheridan got what he really wanted, which was a shot at Jeb Stuart, Lee's dashing cavalry commander. The Union cavalry was ordered out – and good riddance, as far as Meade was concerned – on a raid toward Richmond, which Stuart would be obliged to contest.

On 9 May there was skirmishing between the armies at Spotsylvania, but most of the time was spent entrenching. Lee's lines took shape east to west, where they had fallen in the fighting of 8 May. The result on the Southern side was a large, irregular crescent along the higher ground. Anderson and Jubal Early were on the wings; in the middle, commanded by Richard S Ewell, was a bulging salient dubbed the 'mule shoe.' History would remember it by the name of 'Bloody Angle' from a kink in the salient's line.

Though fighting was light on the 9th, casualties included the much-loved commander of the VI Corps John Sedgwick, who was felled by a sharpshooter just after reassuring a dodging soldier that 'They couldn't hit an elephant at this distance.' Burnside arrived with his division and, in usual

Top: The attack at Spotsylvania Court House.
Above: South view of the Andersonville stockade in 1864. Clara Barton would come here the following year to help identify the Union dead.

Main picture:
Confederate guards fire
on an emaciated Union
prisoner in this 1865
painting of the prison
camp at Andersonville,
whose name was a
synonym for misery.

Inset: The Battle of the
Wilderness, 5-6 May
1864.

A Union drum corps poses stiffly outside its headquarters.

form, gave Grant an incorrect report that Lee was moving north toward Fredericksburg, which was swamped with ever-growing numbers of Union wounded. Grant decided to counter this with a move to Lee's left on the Po River, and late in the day ordered in Hancock's II Corps. On the morning of 10 May Lee discovered Hancock's move on his left and dispatched Heth and Early, who drove Hancock back across the Po with heavy losses. At 4 o'clock in the afternoon Warren met a bloody repulse to the left of the Rebel salient.

Just before dusk, however, came a much more promising development. A young colonel named Emory Upton pursuaded Grant to let him have a try at the salient. Gathering 12 infantry regiments, with reinforcements expected from Gershom Mott's division, Upton led a solid column toward the northwest face of the salient. They discovered the Rebels had fashioned a formidable position indeed – a trench fronted by banked logs, with a head-log on top leaving a space to fire beneath; in front of this parapet was a solid tangle of abatis – felled trees with sharpened limbs.

Upton's men set out at a run across open ground straight at the Southern line. At once a hail of bullets tore into them. The Federal soldiers in front fell in dozens, but somehow a spearhead of them got to the parapet and assaulted the Rebels in the trench, some of the Yankees pitching their bayoneted rifles like harpoons. Incredibly, it worked: the Federals had smashed through the

strongest part of the Confederate line. All they needed now were reinforcements to break Lee's army in two. Mott and his division set out to help as ordered; they were met by a wall of Confederate artillery fire that stopped them in their tracks.

With Southern reinforcements pouring into the breach and his own immobilized, Upton soon realized he was out on a limb. He pulled back with heavy losses, taking with him some 1000 prisoners. But Grant saw that the salient was vulnerable: 'A brigade today – we'll try a corps tomorrow.' He picked Hancock, his most dynamic general and the hero of Gettysburg, to take the battle-honed II Corps down to assault the salient. Federal troop movements took time, so there was little fighting at Spotsylvania on 11 May. The skies clouded over during the day and a steady drizzle began. Grant defiantly wired to Halleck, who was now Chief of Staff, 'I propose to fight it out on this line if it takes all summer.'

Over to the east, Sheridan got his crack at Jeb Stuart that day. In a battle between the opposing cavalries, Stuart was directing his forces when a Federal private got a bead on him at ten yards. Stuart went down mortally wounded. His death (at the age of 31) ended the cavalry superiority that had been a major ingredient in Lee's success. Though the rest of Sheridan's campaign toward Richmond came to little, he had bagged a big prize indeed. On the night of 11 May both armies steeled themselves for the renewal of battle, both knowing that this time no one was going to give in. In Washington, his sleep and all his waking moments haunted by the legions of the dead, Abraham Lincoln read to his friends from Shakespeare's *Macbeth* the lines ending '. . . all our yesterdays have lighted fools the way to dusty death.'

The dawn of 12 May brought a sullen, foggy, drizzly morning. Confederate General Edward Johnson awakened early and inspected his position at the head of the salient. He was extremely worried. A salient was dangerous, especially when held by infantry alone, because its arc created a diverging defensive fire. Salients were workable artillery positions, though – guns could be posted to sweep the sides of the angle and enfilade attackers. What worried Johnson was that the night before Lee had diverted the salient's cannon, its only security, to meet a supposed Federal threat on the right. Johnson was certain that the real attack was gathering out there in the darkness and fog on his front. He had urgently requested return of the cannon, and Lee had agreed. But dawn was almost here: Where were the cannon? He knew that breastwork construction was under way across the base of the salient, but it was far from complete; there was no place to rally. Then he heard a noise and strained to listen in the wet, heavy air. It was cheering in the distance, a jumble of cheering and shouting voices moving toward him. But if it were the attack, why were his pickets not firing? Had they been over-

whelmed in the enemy advance? Johnson glanced back: still no cannon. His men, 5000 strong, awoke and stood to their posts, listening. He peered forward again. Out of the fog rolled a solid wave of blue-clad figures.

The Rebel position erupted into flame, but the hail of bullets could not stop Hancock's 20,000 men. As the Federals in front fell, the human wave rolled over them and crested inexorably onto the breastworks. Before he was captured, Johnson saw his 20 cannon arriving at a gallop – the Federal advance simply swallowed them up.

To the rear, behind his incomplete defensive line at the base of the salient, Robert E Lee sat on his horse and listened. He had heard everything – a furious burst of fire followed by an ominous silence, the silence of catastrophe. The Federals had broken through his line and were now using the bayonet on his men. A broken line could not be held. His army was dying in that silence and haze out there.

Lee spurred his horse over to where his reserves lay, led by General John B Gordon. If Gordon's men could hold off the attack until the new breastworks were ready, the army had a chance. When Lee galloped up, Gordon was already moving to the attack: Lee wheeled and headed for the front of the column. At this moment of supreme danger he intended to head the attack himself. He would lead them to victory or die in the attempt.

Suddenly Gordon's mount blocked his path and

Guards of the 107th Colored Infantry.

Main picture: The Confederate colors triumphant at the Fort Pillow Massacre.
Inset: A Union headquarters in the pine woods.

Above: Men of the 23rd New York Infantry, who voted to include black soldiers in their ranks.

Right: General George B McClellan's secret service was led by Allan Pinkerton (seated in background) who went on to become identified with detective work.

Gordon was seizing the bridle of his horse and shouting 'General Lee, you shall not lead my men! They have never failed you. They will not fail you now!' Soldiers gathered around the two generals, and the murmur among them rose to a cadenced shout: 'General Lee to the rear! General Lee to the rear!' He was their best hope – they would not risk his life.

The men seemed to lift Lee and his horse almost bodily and push them back. Helpless, Lee acquiesced and rode to the rear, turning to shout 'God bless the Virginians!' as the men charged out toward the Federals in the salient. With Gordon, the divisions of Rodes and Ramseur fell like a thunderclap on the disorganized Yankees and herded them back over the breastworks. But there the Federals stayed. They had been routed too many times. Now they had a general who would let them fight and the numbers to win, and they were not going to retreat again. For the Southerners it was a simple equation: the line must be held or all the suffering and dying had been in vain. The line must hold or the war was lost. Upon this mile-wide line two armies concentrated their full might along the same thin parapet, resulting in a day-long, hand-to-hand melee of unbridled ferocity. It was suicide to stay long at that place, but men stayed nevertheless, shooting and stabbing over the breastworks and under the headlogs until they died. They stood and fired until they dropped and their bodies were trampled and shot to pieces. Rain poured down, and the trenches ran with bloodied water. Cannon ran onto the breastworks to shoot directly into the living, dying and

dead a few yards away – artillery charging infantry in a mad inversion. They fired until their crews and carriages were shot away.

At times a soldier would leap onto the breast-works and fire into the enemy, his mates handing him loaded guns until he was shot down and some-one else leaped up. Over the screams and curses, a deep humming sound prevailed over Bloody Angle – the song of tens of thousands of bullets. History had never known such concentrated gunfire at such close range. The breastworks dissolved into splin-ters; behind the line large trees were shattered and felled by musket fire (one reason anyone at all sur-vived was that most were shooting too high). Fight-ing like demons, the soldiers began to resemble demons; their faces black with gunpowder and twisted with agony and rage.

The nightmare lasted some 20 hours. The only lulls had come when both sides stopped firing to throw the dead from the trenches – the bodies im-peded the fighting. Other Federal attacks on both sides of the salient failed during the day. At three o'clock in the morning there was silence at last on Bloody Angle. The Confederates pulled back to the completed breastworks at the base of the salient and the Federals claimed the ghastly parapet and its chest-high heaps of dead and wounded. The enemy line still held as strongly as ever. Nearly 7000 Northerners had fallen, and probably even more Southerners, for that now useless square mile of land.

The battle continued for another seven days, with an abortive major Federal offensive on the 18th, but its fury was spent. Grant slowly slipped his army toward Lee's right, and on 19 May tried again to run around his enemy toward Richmond. Again Lee anticipated the move and won the race. The final convulsion of that terrible campaign came at Cold Harbor, near Richmond, on 3 June. There Grant sent a huge and ill-judged frontal attack onto Lee's entrenchments, during which the North lost another 7000 men in 20 minutes, to no purpose whatever. Throughout the entire war (and into World War I) the leaders of armies had failed to absorb a simple fact of modern warfare that every private knew from bitter experience – well-made breastworks are virtually impregnable to direct assault (though there are exceptions – like the charges on Bloody Angle).

As one observer noted, the Army of the Potomac had 'literally marched in blood and agony from the Rapidan to the James.' For one month the survivors had marched, slept and fought a continuous battle in the same sweat- and blood-stiffened uniforms. There had been 50,000 Union casualties, an average 2000 per day, amounting to 41 percent of the original forces. The South had lost 32,000 – 46 percent – and their losses, unlike the North's, were irreplaceable. Grant had proclaimed he would fight it out all summer, but finally had to face the galling truth: even with twice the men he could not beat

Robert E Lee on the field. He had tried to bludgeon his enemy to death and had failed, because his own army could no longer endure it.

On 7 June Grant issued new orders. Richmond lay to the west, but the Army of the Potomac marched south. Now Grant was going to take the only course he had, one that in the long run was certain to work. He would besiege Petersburg and drain the lifeblood of Lee's Army – if necessary, one drop at a time.

Below: A 900-lb field gun and its crew.

Left: A pre-Civil War volunteer group of the kind that would attract many idealistic young Northerners into combat with the vision of dashing uniforms and heroic deeds.
Following pages: Sherman's March to the Sea.

CHAPTER TEN

TOTAL WAR
SHERMAN'S MARCH TO ATLANTA
AND THE SEA

IN THE SPRING OF 1864, at the same time U S Grant was setting out to challenge Robert E Lee in the East, another part of the Union's grand strategy was rolling into motion in the South. Grant's closest associate in the army, William Tecumseh Sherman, had been ordered 'to move against Johnston's Army, to break it up, and to get into the interior of the enemy's country as far as you can, inflicting all the damage you can against their war resources.'

Sherman's forces, now consisting of three entire armies, lay in Chattanooga, Tennessee. They were the Army of the Cumberland under 'Rock of Chickamauga' George H Thomas; the Army of the Tennessee under James B McPherson; and the Army of the Ohio under John M Schofield – in all, over 100,000 men. Since December they had been gathering for the new offensive into the heart of the Confederacy. Their immediate goal was the critical supply, manufacturing and communications center of Atlanta, Georgia, some 140 miles to the southwest.

The North wanted to conquer Atlanta for more than military reasons. The Union needed a big, decisive victory: there had been none since Chattanooga, and that triumph had left the enemy army intact. And a decisive victory was virtually the only hope for the re-election of Abraham Lincoln over his Democratic challenger, General George B McClellan, who had found better luck in the political arena than in the military. The Democrats vaguely promised some kind of accommodation with the South and thus appealed to the profound war-weariness growing in the North.

These military and political considerations were well understood by Sherman's opponent, General Joseph E Johnston, whose Confederate Army of Tennessee lay south of Chattanooga in Dalton, Georgia. President Jefferson Davis had reluctantly given that command to Johnston after a public clamor following the defeat at Chattanooga had forced the removal of Davis's friend, the incompetent Braxton Bragg. Despite his differences with Davis, Johnston was one of the best generals the South had, and he defined his present goals clearly. He had only 62,000 men and therefore could not immediately take the offensive, especially when the Federals were led by one as able as Sherman. Thus Johnston's tactics must be defensive, resisting Sherman on every foot of ground, forcing him to overextend his supply line and reduce his forces to protect it. When they were reduced, it would be time to take the offensive. Finally, *Atlanta must not fall before the Presidential election*. In sum, Johnston realized his strategy must be Fabian – a fighting retirement over successive positions. This would weaken Sherman for the kill and make it likely that a more accommodating Union President could be elected.

There were two major problems with implementing Johnston's strategy. One was Jefferson Davis, the other a member of his own staff – General John B Hood, who hated defensive strategy of any kind.

The army's other generals – William J Hardee, Leonidas Polk and cavalry leader Joseph Wheeler – would wait and see. As for the Army of Tennessee itself, it was in splendid condition, its equipment and spirit restored by Johnston after the humiliation at Chattanooga.

On 7 May 1864 Sherman's great offensive got under way, his troops probing Confederate positions around Dalton. That morning, as Union troops clashed with the enemy near Ringgold, Georgia, a Federal officer observed 'The ball is opened.' The ensuing campaign to Atlanta was indeed to be like a formal dance, Sherman sweeping to the side of his opposite, Johnston gracefully withdrawing.

On 9 May McPherson's Federal Army flanked Johnston and gained his rear at Snake Creek Gap, threatening Confederate communications at Resaca. On 12 May the Confederates pulled back to strong entrenchments around Resaca, where Sherman mounted three futile attacks against the Rebel lines. At the same time he sent other forces around Johnston's left flank. This dislodged the Confederates three days later. Retiring without haste, they came to a halt farther south at Cassville.

Resaca was the real beginning of the campaign, which became an extraordinary running battle of eight months' duration. As one Confederate participant later commented, 'From then on there was not a day or night, yes, scarcely an hour, that we did not hear the crack of a rifle or the roar of a cannon. To their music we slept, by their thunderings we were awakened.'

So the dance progressed, sashaying southeast around the fulcrum of the Western and Atlantic Railroad toward Atlanta. The Rebels would break up the railroad as they withdrew, the Yankees would

Right: Jefferson Davis's insistence on taking the offensive against Sherman's army contributed heavily to the fall of Atlanta.

repair it as they advanced. From positions at Cassville, Johnston prepared to mount an attack but was dissuaded by Hood and Polk, who claimed they were flanked. The Confederates then withdrew briefly to Allatoona but found Sherman brushing by their left. Sending Wheeler's cavalry to raid Sherman's ever-lengthening supply line, Johnston moved west to positions near Dallas, where beginning on 25 May there was a sharp fight that lasted four days. On the first and third days Sherman assaulted the Confederate entrenchments and lost heavily. On 4 June, however, Johnston realized Sherman was again flanking his left and pulled back to prepared positions at Kennesaw Mountain, near Marietta. Sherman followed and the dance continued with the hellish accompaniment of shot and shell; thus far it had accounted for some 9000 casualties on each side.

Sherman knew well that every step he took made his supply line more tenuous. In early June his cavalry moved east and again secured the railroad, which improved his prospects. (The Civil War was the first in history wherein railroads were essential in moving men and supplies.) But there were threats to Federal supply lines farther back, in Tennessee and Mississippi, centered in the person of Confederate cavalryman Nathan Bedford Forrest, an almost illiterate former slave-trader who had become one of the most brilliant and aggressive generals of the war. (Forrest is known to history for the short summary of military strategy 'Git thar fustest with the mostest' – which apparently he never actually said.)

Sherman declared, with his customary ferocity, 'That devil Forrest . . . must be hunted down and killed if it costs ten thousand lives and bankrupts the Federal Treasury.' In early June Federal cavalry under General S D Sturgis were dispatched to deal with Forrest. In his finest action, commanding less than half Sturgis's numbers, Forrest completely routed the Federals and inflicted enormous losses at Brice's Crossroads, Mississippi (10 May). Union efforts to hunt down 'that devil' were to continue, and to fail, right to the war's end. Nonetheless, Sherman's supplies were never seriously disrupted.

By 14 June Sherman's men were in sight of Johnston's positions on Kennesaw Mountain. That day a Federal artillery battery lobbed a few cannonballs at a Confederate staff conference on Pine Mountain, one of which squarely caught General Polk, killing him instantly. Sherman had only to flank Johnston again to destroy the position. But for some reason, perhaps partly in order to vary his tactics, Sherman decided on an assault. He sent his men sharply uphill into strong works fronted by abatis and swept by crossfire. The result, on 27 June, was a debacle similar in style if not in scale to Grant's at Cold Harbor three weeks before. 'All that was necessary,' one Rebel defender wrote, 'was to load and shoot'; he added, 'I will ever think that the reason they did not capture our works was the impossibility of their living men to pass over the bodies of their dead.' The Federals suffered over 2000 casualties to the South's

442. Yet Sherman scarcely paused to lick his wounds. In a few days he sent McPherson east around Johnston's right flank toward the Chattahoochie River, just northwest of Atlanta.

Failing to anticipate this move was Johnston's first mistake in the campaign. As a result he was forced to withdraw precipitously to the banks of the Chattahoochie, knowing he could not remain there long and that the next stop was Atlanta. This was not his only problem – an increasingly frustrated Davis was pressing him to take the offensive: Johnston was caught between a still impregnable enemy on one side and an implacable commander-in-chief on the other. He had preserved his army and steadily weakened his opponent, had waged a model Fabian campaign and still had Atlanta to fall back on, protected by its elaborate earthworks. There he could likely hold out until the Union elections, or until Sherman gave him an opening. To Davis's constant entreaties, Johnston replied evasively, which was his undoing – and his army's.

Sherman at Kennesaw Mountain, near Marietta, Georgia, 4 October 1864. The disastrous Union attack on impregnable works there led one Confederate defender to recall, 'All that was necessary was to load and shoot.'

On 17 July a telegram arrived from Davis relieving Johnston and giving command of the Army of Tennessee to General John B Hood. It was in essence an order to attack, which was what Hood would certainly do: he was a sad-eyed giant of a man who looked harmless as a teddybear and fought like a wildcat. This had made him an ideal division commander, compensating in boldness for what he lacked in brains. Sherman was as delighted by the appointment as if he had made it himself. Despite having a lamed arm from Gettysburg and a missing leg from Chickamauga, Hood was as aggressive as ever and certain to come out fighting – just what the Federals wanted.

Sherman's three armies converged on Atlanta. Lulled by token resistance, Sherman speculated that Hood, contrary to form, might be evacuating the city. He sent McPherson's Army away on a wide

The Siege of Atlanta.

envelopment to the east, heading for Hood's rail line. The Federals became careless. On the afternoon of 20 July Thomas was moving his army slowly across Peachtree Creek; there was a gap of several miles between his army and those of Schofield and McPherson. It was a serious oversight, but after all, the enemy was supposed to be retreating. In the afternoon the men were resting on the banks of the creek.

Then Hood struck and struck hard, his forces swarming onto the surprised Federals as Jackson had done at Chancellorsville (which seemed to be Hood's great model – though this attack had in fact been planned by Johnston before he was relieved). There was a fierce four-hour fight at close quarters; the Rebels moved around Thomas's right flank, into the gap in the Federal line. For the Federals there was no time to hope for reinforcements. Across the creek, 'Rock of Chickamauga' Thomas found some reserve batteries and began shelling the Confederates along the opposite bank. In Thomas's phrase, that cannonade 'relieved the hitch'; the Rebels fell back. Thomas's men had proved as good as their leader. Both sides had about 20,000 engaged; Confederate losses were some 4800 to about 1800 for the Union. Hood's aggressive strategy thus had a most inauspicious beginning. But the Rebel general was by no means ready to relinquish the initiative, such as it was. Hearing that McPherson's left flank was exposed east of Atlanta and a Federal wagon train vulnerable at Decatur, Hood moved to attack again. While the main body of the Confederates fell back to fortifications around Atlanta, Wheeler was ordered to take his cavalry to Decatur and Hardee to march 15 miles to attack McPherson's flank at dawn. Thus came about the Battle of Atlanta on 22 July.

That morning Hood waited anxiously for the sounds of Hardee's attack. Finally, at about 11:00 AM, he heard the skirmishers open up on the Union left – but apparently in front of McPherson's line, not on the flank as ordered. Hood was furious at this apparent blunder. When Hardee's attack began, Sherman and McPherson were conferring in the middle of the Federal position. Puzzled by the unexpected sound of firing on his front, McPherson leaped onto his horse to investigate. Sherman paced nervously, waiting for news. Shortly an aide dashed up and reported that McPherson's horse had returned bleeding and riderless. McPherson had found Hardee's attack hitting hard, but their attempt to flank him had run afoul of Grenville Dodge's XVI Corps, who were moving into position on the left when the Rebels charged. Thus Hardee had moved as ordered on the enemy flank, but when he got there it was no longer a flank. Dodge's men were pushed back in furious fighting, but put up enough resistance to blunt the attack. McPherson arrived just in time to see a successful countercharge by Ohio regiments. He then dressed his lines and headed to the right to see how the XVII Corps was faring.

McPherson rode right into a group of Confederate skirmishers, who signaled him to surrender. In response, he politely tipped his hat and bolted; immediately he was shot dead from his horse. When his body was brought to Sherman, the general wept openly; at 35, McPherson had been one of the brightest and most promising generals in the army. Command of the Army of the Tennessee was given to General Oliver O Howard, a one-armed veteran of Chancellorsville and Gettysburg.

Confederate cavalry officer John Hunt Morgan, whose unit was celebrated for the endurance, speed and daring of its raids.

Above: Sherman's soldiers receive their pay in captured Atlanta before starting their victorious sweep through the South to the sea.

Below: Sherman's army slogs through high water in South Carolina early in 1865.

Soldiers were wounded and knew it not, so intense was their excitement. Men with shattered fingers changed their muskets to the left hands.

A crisis had arrived. Sherman ordered two batteries to a position commanding a flank fire upon the enemy. The charges of our men were stubbornly resisted, but the determination of the onset overwhelmed everything. Our boys rushed on the enemy's rifle pits, bayoneting them in their works, careless of their own lives as if they had a million souls to spare. . . .

Now came the grand *coup de main*. Two Rebel lines came on exultant and sure of victory. All our artillery was opened upon them. Words cannot describe the awful effects of this discharge: 17,000 rifles and several batteries of artillery, each gun loaded to the muzzle with grape and canister, were fired simultaneously, and the whole center of the Rebel line was crushed down as a field of wheat through which a tornado had passed. The Rebel column gave way, and thus ended the fearful and bloody struggle of the twenty-second of July.

The battle on the Union left was to rage furiously into the evening, but Hardee's men made no headway after their first assault. The Yankees were as determined as their attackers, sometimes meeting and repelling simultaneous attacks on front and rear. Farther to the east, Wheeler had no better luck in his assault on Decatur.

Bitterly disappointed by the lack of success on the Federal left, Hood sent General Benjamin Cheatham's corps to attack the center of the Union line at three o'clock in the afternoon. The Confederates charged to the east along a railroad and punched clear through the Union center, capturing two batteries. A Federal captain would later remember that desperate fighting:

The balance of victory inclined to this side, now to that. Men glared at one another like wild beasts and, when a shell burst among the advancing foe and arms, legs and heads were torn off, a smile of pleasure lighted up our smoke-begrimed faces.

For the second time Hood had failed, his casualties some 8000 of nearly 37,000 engaged, to the North's 3722 of 30,000 engaged. The Confederates had fought the best they knew how, with superior numbers, and failed. It would take as good a general as Sherman to whip the Federals, but Hood knew only how to fight, not how to make plans. Yet he continued to try.

After the battle Atlanta was besieged. On 28 July Sherman ordered Howard's Army to cut the railroad to the south. Hood sent the corps of S D Lee against Howard at Ezra Church; six Rebel assault waves could not rout them but did succeed in keeping the railroad open to Atlanta. Sherman steadily tightened his grip around the city, meanwhile sending more futile sorties against Forrest in Mississippi. He now had command of all the rail lines into Atlanta except the Macon line to the south. In late July 10,000 cavalry under Edward McCook and George Stoneman were sent to raid Macon and cut the railroad. Sherman learned thereby that Hood was still dangerous: McCook's division was routed and dispersed, Stoneman's all but wiped out. For the moment, the Confederates' lifeline stayed open.

In mid-August Hood took the offensive again, making one of the most serious in the chain of blunders that had shattered and demoralized his army. Wheeler's cavalry was ordered to raid Sherman's supply line to the north. The raid lasted a month, but Sherman had already collected all the supplies he needed, and the absence of cavalry fatally weakened Confederate defenses in Atlanta. That fact was not lost on Sherman, who had been waiting for Hood to make the ultimate mistake. This was it.

Leaving a small force before the city, Sherman pulled the armies of Schofield and Thomas from their trenches on 26 August and made a wide sweep around the west of Atlanta, heading for the Macon rail line to the south. Hood concluded the enemy was giving up. Telegrams went out all over the Confederacy: 'The Yankees are gone!' Several railway cars full of ladies arrived in town to assist in the celebration. Hood sent troops south to Jonesboro to hasten his enemy's retreat, but by the end of the 31st the Federals had easily repelled that force and cut the railroad in two places. Atlanta was doomed.

Obtuse as he was, Hood knew the game was up. On 1 September he evacuated Atlanta, blowing up the munitions and stores he could not carry away and heading for entrenchments to the southwest at Lovejoy. Next day the Federals roared into the city and Sherman telegraphed Lincoln 'Atlanta is ours, and fairly won.' The overjoyed President declared a national day of celebration for the victories at Atlanta and Mobile Bay. Privately, he celebrated his own suddenly improved prospects for re-election. With characteristic warmth and wryness, Lincoln wrote to Sherman: 'It is indeed a great success. Not only does it afford the obvious and immediate military advantages, but in showing the world that your army could be divided . . . and yet leaving enough to vanquish Hood's army, it brings those who sat in darkness to see a great light. But what next? I suppose it will be safer if I leave General Grant and yourself to decide.'

Left: Confederate General John Bell Hood, who lost his left leg at Chickamauga but refused to retire. Strapped to his saddle, he led the ill-fated counteroffensive against Sherman's advance to Atlanta. *Below:* Columbia, South Carolina, after its occupation by Sherman's Army.

Main picture: The Battle of Cedar Creek, 19 October 1864.
Inset: An encampment at Yorktown, Virginia, 1864.

Sherman did decide, on a course of action that would make him simultaneously one of the great generals of history and the most hated personage in the long memory of the South. He decreed that the full weight of war was to fall on the civilians of the Confederacy. Atlanta was to become a military camp, its population forcibly evacuated, all buildings of possible military importance destroyed. In short, the city was to be wiped out. Ultimately, only half the civilians were evacuated and his men were ordered not to burn private dwellings, but they often got a little careless with matches: no one was likely to stop them. Sherman wrote to Halleck, 'If the people raise a howl against my barbarity and cruelty, I will answer that war is war, and not popularity seeking. If they want peace, they and their relations must stop the war.' The roads south of the city filled with thousands of exiles who had lost everything but what they could carry with them; they staggered weeping from the burning rubble that had been their homes.

Hood was soon on the road again with his army, heading north to operate against Sherman's supply line in a desperate gamble to force a Federal retreat. First sending Thomas's Army to Nashville on 3 October, Sherman set out in pursuit of Hood, following him back north along his old route. Again Kennesaw Mountain, Allatoona, Resaca and Chattanooga echoed to the sound of gunfire. Then Sherman came to rest in Kingston, Georgia, and

Above: Destroying the railroad at Atlanta.
Right: The elaborate earthworks that failed to save Atlanta from Sherman's Army.

made an historic change of plans. He decided to let Hood go, to let Schofield and Thomas handle him. Hood could not stop him now: Sherman would set out on a gamble of his own. As he and Grant had done in Mississippi on the way to Jackson, he would cut his supply line and march away from Hood, directly across Georgia to the sea. He would show the South and the world that his 60,000 men could go anywhere in enemy territory with impunity. On the way he would take what food his army needed from the people. He would destroy the South's will to resist, would 'make Georgia howl.'

'War,' Sherman wrote, 'like the thunderbolt, follows its own laws and turns not aside even if the beautiful, the virtuous and the charitable stand in its path.' Now the beautiful, the virtuous and the charitable were going to find the war on their own doorsteps. At the time, this was considered barbarism; future generations would call it Total War, and Sherman its first great prophet.

Thus Sherman left Hood to his desperate and ineffectual raids and moved back to Atlanta to complete the work of destruction. On 16 November he set out to the east across the South toward Savannah and the sea. As far as the world was concerned he marched into a hole: there would be no communication. His army was ordered not only to forage off the land but to 'enforce a devastation more or less relentless.' With the air of a holiday rather than a campaign, his army made about ten

Above: Sherman's March set the pattern for the 'total warfare' that would scar the twentieth century. *Left:* Richmond after the Confederate evacuation of April 1865.

Main picture: The Union attack on Fort Fisher, North Carolina, closed the port of Wilmington to Confederate blockade-runners and tightened the stranglehold on the South.
Inset: A pontoon bridge goes into position.

miles a day and spread across a front some 50 miles wide. That front cut through the South like a scythe, leaving a burning and ravaged swath across the rich landscape. On the periphery, like a swarm of locusts, ranged a rabble of deserters – both Yankees and Rebels bonded by a common rapacity. These 'bummers,' as they were called, robbed and burned at random without opposition. Not since the European Thirty Years' War of the 17th century had civilian populations experienced such a reign of terror. Opposing Sherman's march was a motley collection of state militias and Wheeler's Cavalry – some 13,000 in all. Though they forced the Federals to contend with almost constant skirmishing, they could not begin to halt their progress.

Meanwhile, Hood continued haplessly on his way north in Tennessee, battering his army to pieces on the Federal juggernaut. On 30 November he lost 6000 men in attacking Schofield at Franklin. He continued somehow to Nashville, where in mid-December Thomas finally wrecked what little was left of the luckless Confederate Army of Tennessee, which had been hounded to death by President Davis's almost unerring facility for firing good generals and promoting bad ones. After the defeat at Nashville a fleeing Confederate private discovered the gallant, pathetic Hood 'pulling his hair with one hand and crying as if his heart would break. The citizens seemed to shrink and hide from us as we approached them. The once proud Army of Tennessee had degenerated into a mob.' The survivors fled, some to other armies, many to a deserter's safety at home.

On December 10 the world learned that Sherman had emerged unscathed at Savannah. Three days later the Rebel fort outside the city fell; Hardee, in command, evacuated the city on the 21st. Sherman facetiously wired to Lincoln 'I beg to present you, as a Christmas gift, the city of Savannah.' The March to the Sea was accomplished. Sherman prepared to turn north through the Carolinas to join Grant's Army; together they would finish off Lee. The march through the Carolinas was to be another campaign of destruction. The union with Grant would be unnecessary in the end.

William Tecumseh Sherman had fulfilled his task, had mortally wounded the Confederacy's potential for war, had earned the unbridled admiration of the North and the undying hatred of the South. Was his ruthlessness justifiable? History has debated that issue ever since and has resolved nothing. The devastation he set in motion was undeniably excessive and uncontrolled. At the same time, much of the worst of it was contrary to orders, done by stragglers of whom many were Confederate soldiers. On paper, Sherman was ferocious – his letters bristle with threats: 'I shall then feel justified in resorting to the harshest measures, and shall make little effort to restrain my army'; 'Until we can re-populate Georgia, it is useless to occupy it, but the utter destruction of its roads, homes, and people will cripple their military resources'; 'I almost tremble for her [South Carolina's] fate.' Yet none of these threats came fully to pass. By modern standards, his campaign was scarcely a reign of terror at all, since most of the violence and looting fell on property, not persons. There was none of the indiscriminate slaughter of modern guerrilla war and terrorism.

Sherman was a military genius of the first rank. He did his job and did it imaginatively and thoroughly. His ultimate goal had been to hasten the end of the war, and his army's activities were directed toward that purpose. The apparent blind spot in Sherman's moral faculties was shared by later military men who did their jobs equally well and with much greater ruthlessness: their actions came to be considered not barbarism, but normal military procedure – those civilians who happened to be in war's way were simply out of luck.

In the end it could be argued that Sherman was not the real culprit in the March to the Sea, that the true blame lies in the fact put forth succinctly by Sherman himself in the statement: 'War is hell.' From the Civil War onward, that judgment would resonate ever more deeply.

The spectral ruins of Richmond, Virginia, capital of the Confederate States of America.

Petersburg, Virginia, the railway center essential to supplying Lee's Army. In the summer of 1864, the city had only 2500 defenders.

CHAPTER ELEVEN
PETERSBURG
THE LONG DAYS TO VICTORY

Below: Confederate aristocrat Wade Hampton, a brigadier general who helped defend Richmond .
Bottom: Columbia in flames.
Opposite page: Union General Winfield Scott Hancock.

BY THE SUMMER OF 1864, the Confederacy was sinking into defeat. It had lost most of its vital cities and ports, a substantial number of its men and its grip on the oppressive slave-labor system that had supported its economy. Already there was serious talk of enlisting freed slaves in the Confederate Army, which was a manifestly desperate course. (In the North the Thirteenth Amendment, abolishing slavery as an institution, was in preparation.)

Yet the Rebels fought on, with all the valor and resourcefulness that hungry and half-naked men could muster against a well-fed, well-outfitted and increasingly more numerous enemy – the tangible embodiment of an industrial might that was assuming prominence on the world's stage. Time and time again in the summer of 1864, though, that Northern juggernaut had crashed and halted before Robert E Lee's band of starving men, who never stopped fighting long enough to consider how hopeless was their cause.

The Union Army of the Potomac had been stymied in the Wilderness, at Spotsylvania and at Cold Harbor. When U S Grant changed his tactics in June, ordering his army south, away from Richmond, it was partly an admission of short-term defeat and partly an assumption of victory in the long run. He would besiege Petersburg, a rail center through which flowed the food and supplies Lee's army lived and fought on. When Petersburg fell, both Richmond and Lee would be finished, and so would the Confederacy.

Grant was at his best in making large strategic movements, campaigns involving great numbers of men and materiel – war by maneuver. His turning movement was one of the masterpieces of his career. The 100,000 men of the Army of the Potomac pulled out of their trenches in front of Cold Harbor and swung south seemingly without a sound, screened by Warren's cavalry in front and with Philip Sheridan raiding on a diversion around Charlottesville. For once, Lee was fooled. He remained on guard in Richmond. By 16 June the entire Federal Army had crossed the James River on an enormous pontoon bridge and was threatening Petersburg; despite repeated warnings, Lee did not discover the enemy's move until the 18th.

The warnings came from the Confederate commander in the area, General P G T Beauregard, another able Southern general who had incurred the ire of Jefferson Davis and spent much of the war out of the main action. For a month Beauregard had kept the army of blundering General Ben Butler bottled up in the Bermuda Hundred, a peninsula between the James and Appomattox Rivers just northeast of Petersburg. By 14 June Beauregard knew Grant was headed for Petersburg, but could not convince Lee of it. The city had only 2500 defenders; the rest of Beauregard's army was occupied with Butler. Grant knew well how vulnerable the city was: on 15 May he ordered General William F ('Baldy') Smith to move his 16,000 men down from Bermuda Hundred and assault the city, supported by two divisions of Winfield S Hancock's II Corps. Petersburg was then wholly at their mercy.

But on that 15 June a spirit of confusion and indecisiveness began creeping into the Union command structure, a spirit that was to grow and fester for the duration of the campaign. Hancock's orders from Grant were vague; he hardly knew what he was marching to do, and bad maps got him lost repeatedly. 'Baldy' Smith dallied, finally getting his attack

Savannah, Georgia, ultimate objective of Sherman's March to the Sea.

under way at seven in the evening. It made quick progress, as was inevitable against such slim defenses – trenches were swamped, guns and hundreds of prisoners captured. Eventually Hancock arrived, his men smelling victory and ready to join Smith and march into Petersburg. Then, in one of the supreme blunders of the war, 'Baldy' Smith decided he'd rather not press the attack. It was past dark. He would let the men rest and do it tomorrow.

The Federal soldiers were by no means grateful – though Beauregard certainly was. Around the Northern campfires that night echoed, as one soldier recalled, 'the most bloodcurdling blasphemy I ever listened to . . . uttered by men who knew they

Left: Recruits for the Union Army on New York's Beekman Street. Black soldiers were actively recruited in the North from 1863 onward.

Entrenchments for the siege of Petersburg.

Above: Ruins of the Norfolk Navy Yard.
Right: Confederate General Jubal A ('Jubilee') Early threatened Washington in 1864, but was driven back to the Shenandoah Valley where Sheridan outgeneraled him.
Opposite page: Robert E Lee, who fought a masterly defensive campaign against hopeless odds.

were to be sacrificed on the morrow.' The Army of the Potomac had outgeneraled its generals again: they knew they could virtually have ended the war that night, and that tomorrow would be too late.

Pulling most of his men out of Bermuda Hundred, Beauregard had 14,000 defenders in the city by the morning of 16 June. Reinforcements were on the way from Lee, who was beginning to wonder if Beauregard might be right about Grant's whereabouts. During the day the bulk of the Army of the Potomac began arriving, and Grant sent assaults against the city. But on that and the two succeeding days they made no headway and suffered heavy losses. On the 17th the Confederates actually gained back some ground, and that night Beauregard pulled his lines back to tighter and stronger trenches around the city. By the 18th the Federal offensive had succumbed to a growing disorganization that prompted a livid Meade to write his commanders: 'I find it useless to appoint an hour to effect cooperation. What additional orders to attack you require I cannot imagine.'

That day the Army of Northern Virginia began to

arrive in the city. Lee had at last realized his mistake, though the Federals had given him plenty of time to rectify it. Now the city was virtually immune to direct assault. The Union soldiers knew it even if their leaders did not – ordered to charge during the assaults of the 18th, a veteran told a gunner, 'We are going to run toward the Confederate earthworks and then we are going to run back. We have had enough of assaulting earthworks.'

In four days of fighting the North had lost 11,386 casualties of 63,797 engaged; Confederate losses are unknown (41,499 were engaged), but they must have been far smaller. As at Vicksburg, Grant had begun by trying to avoid a siege, but was forced to settle for the inevitable. The main Confederate entrenchments surrounded Petersburg in a large east-west arc, both ends resting on the Appomattox River, which was protected against Union ships by cannon. Grant's lines took shape to the east, and over the next months slowly crept to the west around the city. On 22-23 July the Federals made a sortie against the Weldon Railroad south of Peters-

Opposite page: Union General Ambrose E Burnside, whose career was wrecked by the ill-judged mine assault at Petersburg, where many Federal troops were slaughtered in the crater made by the explosion. *Below:* The McLean House, Appomattox Court House, Virginia.

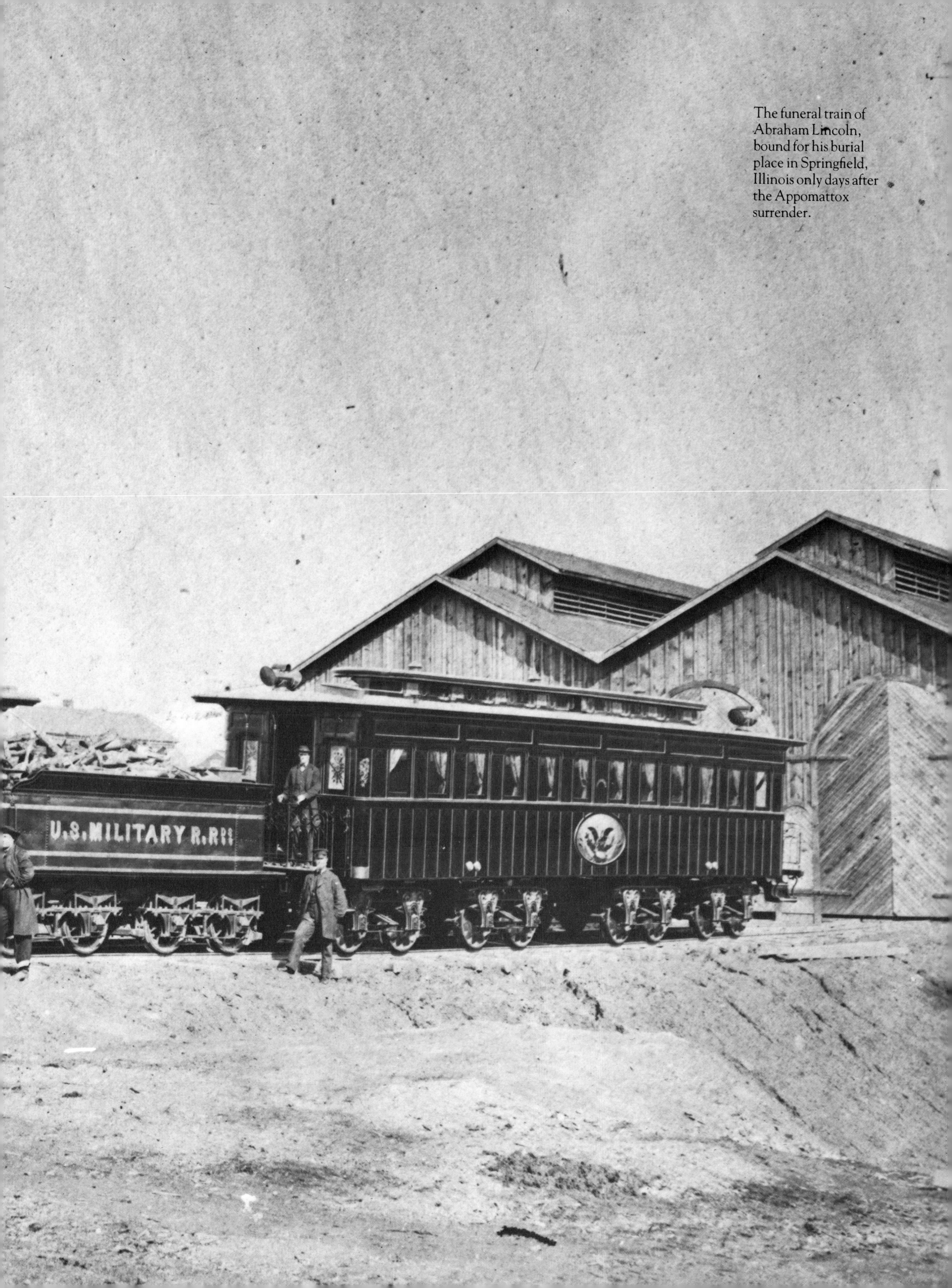

The funeral train of
Abraham Lincoln,
bound for his burial
place in Springfield,
Illinois only days after
the Appomattox
surrender.

burg, but A P Hill's men pushed them back. Meanwhile, Confederate General Jubal Early had mounted a raid toward Washington that threw the capital into a panic and brought his forces to the very gates of the city before he fell back on 11 July. Early's purpose, of course, was to draw away Grant's men from Petersburg. Knowing, or at least hoping that Washington was strong enough, Grant did not take the bait. Lee was his only objective.

There was another Federal offensive around Petersburg during July, one that would cap the military career of the genial and inept Ambrose E Burnside. It is perhaps significant that the two most incompetent Union generals of the war, Burnside and Ben Butler, were both attracted to novel methods of warfare. One of Butler's pet ideas, the wire entanglements used at his otherwise deplorable Drewry's Bluff action – from which he retreated to Bermuda Hundred – was at least effective. Burnside's fancy had been caught by one Colonel Henry Pleasants, who had been a mining engineer before

the war. Pleasants had formulated a plan to dig a 510-foot tunnel under the Confederate trenches at Elliot's Salient, just east of the city. Grant and Meade were distinctly cool to the notion, but approved it mainly to keep Burnside and his men out of trouble. On 25 June, 400 former Pennsylvania coal miners went to work. By 23 July the tunnel, of unprecedented length in military history, was completed, and workers began placing hundreds of barrels of black powder in magazines dug under the Confederate parapets. Burnside had not neglected to prepare troops for this unusual duty. The division of General Edward Ferrero had spent a month training for the attack. They had been picked supposedly because they were the freshest troops in the army. They also happened to be a black division.

Black troops had been actively recruited in the North since 1863; by the end of the war they numbered about 300,000, many of them former slaves. Their progress in the Union Army had been attended by all the racism then prevalent in the

From Five Forks to Appomattox, drawn by R F Zogbaum.

3242

North as well as the South. Their fighting ability had been maligned, until they had repeatedly proved they could fight as well as whites (their officers were almost entirely white). In the army they remained a touchy subject, a problem close to the core of the entire American dilemma.

On 30 July the show was ready to begin. However, the day before, Meade with Grant's approval had ordered a change in plans: the black division was not to lead the attack – if it failed, public opinion might accuse the Union of callously misusing its black soldiers (which, given the experimental nature of the operation, was very possibly the case). After this rebuff, Burnside seemed listless and indifferent, simply drawing straws to see whose division would lead the attack. James H Ledlie, commanding the I Division, lost. Burnside must **have** known this was the weakest division in the

army and Ledlie the least experienced general, but it did not seem to bother him. Furthermore, Burnside was vague in giving his final instructions: Ledlie rounded up his men with only a very hazy idea of what they were supposed to do.

The explosion was planned for 3:30 in the morning on the 30th. At that moment all eyes strained toward the Rebel parapet. Ledlie's division waited in the trenches, but nothing happened. It was discovered that the long fuse had fizzled, and it was relit. At 4:45 AM one of the largest explosions ever seen on the American continent sent flames, earth, cannons, Confederates, and parts of Confederates a hundred feet into the air in the midst of a mushroom-shaped cloud. When it had all settled, there was a gigantic crater 170 feet long, 60 to 80 feet wide and 30 feet deep stretching well into the Southern position.

A Richmond street in 1865, burned out by Confederate forces before they evacuated the city.

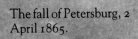

The fall of Petersburg, 2
April 1865.

For the time being the surviving Rebel defenders had fled the area. Terrified by the blast, so had Ledlie's division. It took ten minutes to get them back in position to advance, at which point it was discovered that no provision at all had been made to get them out of the trenches, which were quite deep. They scrambled up as best they could, already considerably disorganized, and then stopped around the crater to gawk at the appalling mess within. With some prodding, the I Division began jumping and sliding into the hole. Finding themselves in a morass of pits and house-high blocks of clay, they stumbled in confusion toward the other end. Meanwhile Ledlie, their commander, cowered in a bombproof shelter behind Union lines, consoled by a jug of rum.

Soon the Southerners collected their wits and began to train their artillery and muskets into the hole. Finding themselves relatively sheltered in the crater, the ostensible attackers were even less disposed to climb out of it. By the time 15,000 men had

Sheridan's Ride through the Shenandoah Valley before the Battle of Cedar Creek.

been herded into the crater the enemy fire had become truly murderous and the Federals were interested solely in hiding. The Union Army was now literally at the feet of the enemy.

Finally, in desperation, Burnside ordered in the black division originally slated to lead the attack. After dispatching them, their commander, Ferrero, joined Ledlie in the bombproof shelter. The black soldiers advanced resolutely and alone and were cut to pieces on the other end, though not before somehow taking 250 prisoners. Firing into the huddled masses of Federals, the Confederates screamed, 'Take the white man – kill the nigger!' The whole inglorious affair ended with a confused melee of surviving Federals rushing devil-take-the-hindmost back to their own lines. The North lost 3748 casualties of 20,708 engaged – about a third of them from the black division; the South lost about 1500 of 11,466.

Grant called the Petersburg mine assault a 'stupendous failure,' while admitting that if the black troops had led the attack as planned it would probably have succeeded. Lincoln's reported reaction was an historic epitaph to the unique military career of Ambrose E Burnside: 'Only Burnside could have managed such a coup, wringing one last spectacular defeat from the jaws of victory.'

With the mine disaster to crown his reign of error, Burnside was cashiered for the second and final time and retired to a successful life in politics. Military history would remember him with fondness as perhaps the worst general ever, but in all other respects a genuinely likeable person.

The siege of Petersburg continued, day on day, month on month. In its first weeks there had been no rain, and a choking cloud of dust hung everywhere. Later weeks brought too much rain; the men in the trenches stood all day in waist-high water. Snipers waited in readiness for those careless enough to show their heads. Every day a battle raged somewhere; cannon and mortars roared incessantly (the soldiers hated the mortars most – they could drop shells unexpectedly straight into the trenches). The Federals gradually inched around the city, moving steadily toward the Confederate lifelines of the railroads.

On both sides the trenches were much the same – on the side facing the enemy would be a wall of logs with earth in front and sandbags on top, leaving gaps for firing. Within the lines were bombproof shelters dug into the earth and strongly roofed. Before the embankment was a ditch about six feet deep, in front of which lay abatis – or *chevaux-de-frise* – logs bristling with six-foot sharpened stakes. In front of all were stations for pickets and sharpshooters. At intervals along the lines were forts, square enclosures of logs and earth housing cannon. Needless to say, these works were not easily to be assaulted. So men sat in them through the months and languished and died a few at a time. At some point someone observed to Grant that the two armies were like the Kilkenny cats that devoured each other tail first. 'Our cat has the longer tail,' Grant bluntly replied.

The Army of the Potomac was hardly the same force that had set out in May. Subjected to three months of the hardest and most deadly fighting in American history, it had lost well over half its veterans in casualties over the summer of 1864. Many famous units, like the Iron Brigade, had virtually ceased to exist. The fabled II Corps, which began the summer with 6799 men, had suffered 7970 casualties, including 40 regimental commanders. Yet that corps and the whole army stayed more or less at strength, thanks largely to the draft and to enlistment bounties that kept personnel in the trenches but by no means guaranteed good soldiers. And the sullen waiting and ducking of trench warfare was poor training for an army of recruits.

The rigors of the campaign and the siege had their effect on the Northern command structure as well. Meade was more irascible than ever, and his relations with Grant – which so far had been surprisingly good – began to deteriorate to the extent that Grant considered relieving him. Hancock, the best fighting general in the army, was troubled and demoralized by his old Gettysburg wound and by the strain of constant fighting; he quarreled with John Gibbon,

President Lincoln's first cabinet and his trusted military advisers.

The James Bennett House, where Johnston surrendered to Sherman.

his best division commander. Lee's army was also devastated, and hungrier and shabbier than ever. They were nearly all veterans, for the simple reason that there were few recruits to be found. For all their experience, however, hunger, exhaustion, disease and desertion had taken their toll. The army was by no means capable of the heroics of its recent past; indeed, it was hardly capable of taking the offensive at all. The weight of the North was slowly squeezing the life out of the Army of Northern Virginia.

In August of 1864 Grant sent General Gouverneur K Warren to try again to seize the Weldon Railroad south of Petersburg. The Federals occupied the line on the 18th, and two attacks by A P Hill could not dislodge them, though the North lost 4455 casualties to the South's 1600. Now only one Confederate lifeline was left – the South Side Railroad on the west.

In September Grant sent 'Phil' Sheridan with infantry and cavalry on a campaign into the Shenandoah Valley of Virginia, which would become nearly as famous as Stonewall Jackson's operations there in 1862. Sheridan had two goals. First, he was to drive out Jubal Early, whose army had retired there after the raid on Washington. Second, he was to make quite sure the valley would send no more food and forage to Confederate Armies. Grant's instructions were ruthless: devastation was to be so complete that a crow flying over the valley would have to carry its own provisions.

Sheridan proceeded to turn the fertile, beautiful Shenandoah Valley into a smouldering ruin. In the process he dealt harshly with Jubal Early, defeating him at Winchester and Fisher's Hill in mid-September. On 19 October Early's men suddenly attacked and routed the Federals at Cedar Creek while Sheridan was away. Arriving and riding furiously through his fleeing troops, Sheridan turned them around and swamped Early's army. It was the last significant Rebel resistance in the valley, which had been the breadbasket of the Confederacy. (Sheridan's ride to Cedar Creek was to be immortalized, with appropriate exaggeration, in a famous poem.)

Sheridan then pursued his course through the Shenandoah Valley like an avenging angel. A small but volatile man of manic ferocity in battle, Sheridan drove his men and officers almost as hard as he drove the enemy. An admiring subordinate called him 'that form of condensed energies'; to the Rebels, he was 'Sheridan the Inevitable.'

On 8 November Abraham Lincoln was re-elected to a second term as President by a substantial majority over his opponent, General George B McClellan. Significantly, for all their affection for 'Little Mac,' the military vote went overwhelmingly to Lincoln. The doubts felt by many civilians in the North about the President's war policy were clearly not shared by the army.

General Philip
Sheridan's charge at the
Battle of Five Forks,
Virginia, 1 April 1865.

In mid-January 1865, after a bungled attempt by Ben Butler that got him fired at last, Admiral David Dixon Porter took Fort Fisher on the coast of North Carolina, the last port held by the Confederacy for its blockade-runners, and virtually its last link to the outside world. Now the South was alone.

In February Grant extended his lines to Hatcher's Run, south of Petersburg. Sherman, meanwhile, was fighting and burning his way north through the Carolinas toward union with the Army of the Potomac. If Sherman effected that union, Lee's army had not a chance in the world. Shattered and tired as the Confederates were, they had to try something; the only choices left were those of desperation.

At length Lee decided to try and get part of his army to Carolina to join forces with Joe Johnston, who was incapable of resisting Sherman alone. Perhaps together they could deal with Sherman and then turn to defeat Grant.

The Southern attempt to break out of Petersburg came on 25 March at Fort Stedman, east of the city. Lying 150 yards from the Confederate position, it was the weakest part of the Federal line. Lee hoped to break through here and strike the Federal com-

Right: The Emancipation Proclamation of 1863, which declared that 'All persons held as slaves within said designated States, and parts of States, are, and henceforward shall be free.'
Below: General Robert E Lee, respected by all who knew him, would become a symbol of the ultimate reconciliation between North and South.

munications, thereby forcing Grant to pull troops from farther south and leave an opening in his line through which Lee could send forces south to Johnston.

In the early morning, Federals at Fort Stedman were surprised and quickly overwhelmed by the Confederates; the Rebel infantry was swarming down the Union trenches and into the Federal rear before any resistance was mounted. For an hour or so it seemed like old times. But then a counterattack by six new Pennsylvania regiments, commanded by General John Hartranft, brought the Confederate advance to a halt. At eight o'clock Lee called off the attack. It was the last great offensive of the Army of Northern Virginia. The next day Lee notified President Davis that his position in Petersburg was no longer tenable, given the approach of Sherman, and that the Confederate Government had best consider pulling out of Richmond. Simultaneously, Sheridan's Federal forces arrived back from their devastation of the Shenandoah Valley, ready to join in the last battle.

For Robert E Lee, for the Army of Northern Virginia, for the Confederate States of America, the incredible was about to happen. After all the glorious speeches, the fatuous defenses of slavery, the gallant fighting and the victories, the unforeseen and terrible suffering and dying, the gaunt and humiliating specter of final defeat was at their door. Robert E Lee was far from a loser, but he had lost. His ranks and his command structure were decimated: Jackson, Stuart, dozens of other generals were dead. The Army of Northern Virginia had been one of the most remarkable fighting forces in history but they had lost. Now they had only to play out their role to the final curtain.

It happened with bewildering speed. On 29 March Grant sent cavalry and infantry under Sheridan and Warren southwest to envelop the Confederate right flank. Lee dispatched 10,000 men under George Pickett to stop them. The Federal operation was slowed by heavy rains and Rebel resistance, but Sheridan was implacable: vowing the rain would not stop his cavalry, he shouted, 'I'm ready to strike out tomorrow and go to smashing things!'

On 31 March Sheridan assaulted Pickett around Dinwiddie Court House; outnumbered five to one, Pickett's force fought for hours before pulling back to Five Forks. Lee sent a desperate message to Pickett to hold that position 'at all costs'; if it fell, the South Side Railroad, the last lifeline, was doomed. But on 1 April Sheridan, seemingly everywhere on the field at once with his battle flag, overpowered the Confederates at Five Forks and captured nearly half of them. Many of the rest fled the war back to their homes. (In spite of his victory, Sheridan cashiered Warren on the spot for moving too slowly. Warren was vindicated years later, but his career was ruined.)

Now Lee had to get out. He notified Davis on 2 April that he would evacuate Petersburg. Grant, determined above all else not to let Lee escape again, unleashed a stupendous artillery barrage on the whole length of the Confederate line, and fol-lowed it with an attack by the VI Corps, who broke through the Rebel right. In the fighting, A P Hill, who had saved the Confederacy at Antietam and had been at Lee's side through all the victories, was killed. The news visibly staggered Lee.

During the day the Confederate Government fled Richmond. Warehouses and arsenals were set afire, the flames spreading into the city. Lee pulled out that night and marched his exhausted and starving army west toward Amelia Court House, hoping to put them on the Danville Railroad to the Carolinas. On 3 April Federal soldiers occupied Petersburg and Richmond. The next day the Confederate capital saw the lanky form of Abraham Lincoln, surrounded by cheering slaves, striding through the streets. At last Lincoln sat pondering at the desk of Jefferson Davis.

If defeat seemed incredible to the Confederate Army, the prospect of victory after so many dis-appointments was equally incredible to Union soldiers. News of the fall of Richmond was received at first with derision: they had heard that one before. No sooner had they absorbed the reality than they were on the road in the final race with the enemy. Sheridan had anticipated Lee's march to Amelia Court House, and rode to cut off the Danville Rail-road. Lee's army was now surrounded – Meade's infantry was on the east and Sheridan on the south and west. Escape to the north was impossible. Lee

Lee's surrender to Grant at the McLean House, Appomattox Court House, Virginia.

the fox was being run to earth by Sheridan the hound. Rebel soldiers were deserting in hundreds. 'My God!,' cried Lee, 'Is the army dissolved?'

Denied the railroad by Sheridan, Lee marched again on 5 April. Next day his army divided by accident into two segments. Led by Sheridan's dismounted cavalry, the Federals fell on one of the wings at Saylor's Creek and captured 8000, one-third of the remaining Rebel strength. The pathetic remains of the Army of Northern Virginia limped on to the west, harried incessantly by Federal cavalry. Then on 9 April Lee found Sheridan the Inevitable blocking his path at Appomattox Court House. It was the end.

But still the shadow of that great army could not die without a fight. Lee sent cavalry around the Federal right flank and infantry and artillery under John B Gordon broke through the center of Sheridan's line. For a brief moment there was open country in front of the Army of Northern Virginia. Then from over the hill appeared Union infantry, line after line of blue.

The firing died down. For the last time the two armies surveyed one another across the battlefield. Then Sheridan sounded his bugles for the charge. But before the Federals could fall upon the ragged Confederates, a horseman appeared galloping furiously from behind Southern lines. He carried a white flag.

The war was over, and it was not over. Lee's surrender to Grant at Appomattox on 9 April almost ended the hostilities (Johnston surrendered to Sherman on the 18th). But the assassination of Lincoln on 14 April was only the first of the aftershocks that would shake American society: the Civil War would never leave the consciousness of the nation.

Lincoln above all had tried to see beyond the immediate business and horror of the war to the deeper questions: What good could come out of this suffering? What did it all mean? In the Gettysburg Address he had dealt with the first question. The 'honored dead,' 'those who gave their lives that this nation might live,' were the dead of both sides: Lincoln prophesied that the nation that would arise from the war, purged by great suffering of slavery and sectionalism, would be stronger and greater than ever before. In this prophecy he was to prove right.

The second question, the meaning of the war, the meaning of great wars themselves, Lincoln spoke of in his Second Inaugural Address. There he was obliged to admit that the question defeated him, that the causes and meaning of such gigantic scourges are beyond human comprehension.

Below: The Confederate battle flag furled for the last time.

Right: Planning the peace, before the traumatic assassination of Abraham Lincoln on 14 April 1865.

INDEX

Page numbers in italics refer to illustrations

Acknowledgments

The publisher would like to thank
the following people who have
helped in the preparation of this
book: Ron Callow, who designed it;
Robin L Sommer, who edited it;
John K Crowley, who did the picture
research; Cynthia Klein, who
prepared the index.

Picture Credits

Bison Picture Library: 11 (top left),
    90, 140
Brown University Library: 16
    (above), 19 (bottom), 22, 74–5,
    98, 122–3, 139 (inset), 150–51,
    158 (inset), 182–3
Chicago Historical Society: 9 (top
    right), 11 (center), 30 (bottom),
    36 (top right), 44 (top), 50, 62
    (top), 77 (bottom), 78, 84, 92–3,
    100–101, 108 (top), 111 (center),
    112–13, 173

Harper's Weekly: 68 (all), 69, 83
    (bottom), 145 (above), 164
    (bottom)
Historical Society of Atlanta: 23
    (both)
Kurz & Allison: 2–3, 6–7, 14–15, 18
    (top), 51 (bottom), 52–3, 64–5,
    71 (top) 79 (top), 102–03, 110–
    111 (bottom), 114–15, 118–19,
    119 (inset), 126–7, 134–5, 138–
    9, 142–3, 154–5, 158–9, 178–9,
    186–7, 190 (above)
Library of Congress: 1, 4–5, 8 (left),
    9 (top left and bottom), 11 (top
    right, bottom right), 12–13, 12
    (above), 13 (top right), 16
    (bottom), 18 (bottom), 19
    (center), 20 (top), 21 (both), 24,
    26, 27 (both), 28–9, 30 (top), 31

(bottom), 33 (all), 34, 35, 36 (top
    left, bottom), 37, 38 (both), 40,
    41 (bottom), 42 (both), 43
    (both), 44–5, 46, 47 (above), 48–
    9, 51 (top), 54, 55, 56–7, 58
    (both), 59, 60, 62 (bottom), 66,
    67 (both), 70 (both), 71 (below),
    72–3, 76 (bottom), 81, 85
    (above), 86 (above), 87 (top,
    bottom, left and right), 88–9, 91,
    96, 97, 104, 105 (top), 107, 108
    (bottom), 109, 110 (left), 116,
    120 (both), 121, 124 (both), 125,
    128, 129 (all), 130–31, 132
    (both), 133, 136, 141, 143
    (inset), 145 (below), 148, 151
    (right), 152 (top), 153 (both),
    156 (both), 157 (both), 160–61,
    162–3, 164 (above), 165, 166–7,
    168–9 (both), 170 (both), 171,
    172, 174–5, 177, 180–81 (both),
    184, 185, 188 (both), 189
Musée de l'Armée: 11 (bottom left)
National Archives: 13 (top right),
    19 (top), 39, 144 (both)
National Portrait Gallery: 10, 25
New York Historical Society: 31
    (top)
New York Public Library: 8 (right),
    20 (right), 87 (center), 95, 105
    (bottom), 117, 148 (inset), 137
    (both), 149
US Army Photograph: 41 (top), 47
    (below), 61, 94, 99, 106, 176
US Naval Historical Center: 17, 20
    (center), 63, 73 (top), 76
    (above), 77 (top and center), 79
    (bottom), 80 (both), 82 (both),
    83 (top), 85 (bottom), 86
    (bottom), 152 (bottom)
Virginia State Library: 32
White House Collection: 190
    (bottom)